Yogurt Every Day

Yogurt Every Day

Healthy and Delicious Recipes for
Breakfast, Lunch, Dinner, and Dessert

HUBERT CORMIER

Nutritionist/Dietitian

appetite
by RANDOM HOUSE

Library and Archives of Canada Cataloguing in Publication is available upon request.
ISBN: 978-0-14-753042-4
eBook ISBN: 978-0-14-753043-1

Recipe photographer: Catherine Côté
Portrait photographer: Francis Fontaine
Food styling: Hubert Cormier and Catherine Côté
Printed and bound in China

Published in Canada by Appetite by Random House®
a division of Penguin Random House Canada Limited

www.penguinrandomhouse.ca

10 9 8 7 6 5 4 3 2 1

appetite
by RANDOM HOUSE | Penguin
Random
House

Table of Contents

"The table is a matchmaker of friendships."

–French proverb

Breakfast

Lunch

Dinner

Snacks

Dessert

Introduction

I like to have fun in the kitchen. I like to discover new foods and new culinary techniques and to build on this knowledge to delight my family and friends. Cooking, to me, means gathering with loved ones around the kitchen island, chatting and drinking wine while a piece of meat braises in the oven and dessert sets in the refrigerator. It also means comforting my best friend who just got separated or an aunt who's in mourning. And, of course, cooking means indulging myself and eating what makes me happy. Food gathers you, me, and everyone around the same table.

So why a yogurt cookbook? As part of my PhD, my thesis advisor asked me if I was interested in writing a paper on yogurt consumption and cardiometabolic risk factors. It wasn't my field of study—which is genetics and nutrigenomics—but I was interested in the idea. I started to review the literature that links yogurt and good health. As my research progressed, I found some interesting results showing that people who consumed yogurt had better prudent dietary pattern scores than those who didn't. The prudent diet protects against heart disease and focuses on eating fruits, vegetables, nuts, fish, and lean meats (among other things) rather than a lot of refined products and sugar, as is commonly observed in the Western dietary pattern. As my team and I researched, we realized that yogurt is the only dairy product included in the prudent dietary pattern. We eventually published our study in the *European Journal of Nutrition*, but I wanted to keep working on yogurt!

In *Yogurt Every Day*, you'll find more than 75 recipes that span breakfast, lunch, dinner, and dessert, as well as some amazing snack ideas. Yogurt is an interesting and versatile food that can help you reduce the fat content of your meal without noticing a difference in taste or texture. It also helps increase your protein intake, especially if you're using Greek yogurt. My goal with this book is to help you create not only delicious meals, but also full and wonderful gastronomic experiences. You'll find healthy versions of my favorite dishes, which include cakes, pavlova, pasta, and some decadent breakfasts.

Are all of the recipes "healthy"? Yes! I provide nutritional value information because it can be helpful to those who must abide by a special diet, such as those with diabetes. But my definition of eating well includes listening to yourself, cooking with fresh ingredients, and having fun.

Welcome to my table, where yogurt is a favorite guest!

Hubert

2,000 BC

In Persia and India, yogurt was used as a preservative for milk. Yogurt, which is slightly acidic, helped prevent milk from spoiling and fought the development of pathogenic microorganisms responsible for many diseases. Yogurt was also used as an ingredient in many recipes.[2]

AD 1072

Turks were the first people to use yogurt for medicinal purposes, as a cure against various illnesses and symptoms such as stomach upset and sunburns. Yogurt was also used as a household product and beauty lotion.[4]

5,000 BC

In the Middle East, shepherds stored milk in bags made of goatskin. After being transported for hours by camels under the hot desert sun, the milk would transform into a soured cream. The traces of gut juices left over in the bag's material, combined with the heat and the movement from the camel's steps, provided the required conditions to transform milk into yogurt.[1]

AD 75

The oldest writings containing the word "yogurt" are attributed to Pliny the Elder, who was born Gaius Plinius Secundus in AD 23 in Como, Italy, and died in AD 79 during the eruption of Mount Vesuvius, close to Pompeii. A writer and naturalist, Pliny the Elder noticed that some nomadic tribes knew how to "thicken milk to turn it into a substance with a pleasing tartness."[3]

AD 1905

At 27 years old, medical student Stamen Grigorov discovered a strain of bacillus responsible for fermenting milk, allowing it to become yogurt. Today, this bacterium is known as *Lactobacillus delbrueckii* (or until 2014 known as *Lactobacillus bulgaricus*), and it is still used in the production of yogurt.

AD 1542

King Francis I of France began importing yogurt to Europe after it cured him of severe stomach upset.

Today

Yogurt is commonly sold in supermarkets around the world. It is part of our daily lives, and recent studies have shown that people who eat yogurt generally have a better diet profile and healthier lifestyle than those who do not.

Health Benefits

YOGURT AND PROTEINS

Your body needs proteins. Proteins not only help build muscles but also contribute to the creation of antibodies that protect you in case of infection or illness. The proteins we eat are transformed into amino acids, which are organic compounds that exist in 22 variations that combine to form new types of proteins. The sequencing of amino acids is crucial to the creation of new proteins because it determines their roles and functions.

Consequently, your diet should provide a sufficient amount of protein, and the official daily recommendation is 0.8 grams per kilogram (0.37 grams per pound) of body weight. For example, a woman weighing 70 kilograms (about 155 pounds) should eat a minimum of 56 grams (2 ounces) of protein per day. The daily amount differs for those who regularly practice sports because an additional intake of protein is recommended to rebuild muscle fibers. In such cases, 1.2 grams per kilogram (0.56 grams per pound) of body weight is ideal. The diet of some athletes and bodybuilders features even more daily proteins, but a high intake of protein increases your daily energy intake and can lead to weight gain if you're not exceptionally active. Moreover, over time, too much protein can damage kidney functions by overloading them. On the contrary, an insufficient protein intake could lead to failure to develop muscle mass, edema, dull skin, or thin and brittle hair.

Greek yogurt has a much higher protein content than other types of yogurt because of the way it is made. To make Greek yogurt, you need three times the amount of milk that is required to make regular yogurt, and the product is strained, which concentrates the protein levels. I recommend having Greek yogurt for breakfast because it can be difficult to find ways to consume the required amount of protein in the morning. Plus, eating more protein in the morning helps fight hunger pangs throughout the day. In fact, researchers have discovered that, compared with people eating a traditional breakfast (with 10 percent of calories coming from proteins), those who have a protein-rich breakfast (with 25 percent of calories coming from proteins) show a lower overall appetite. Regulating one's appetite also positively affects hormonal balance, which could partly explain the importance of a protein-rich breakfast.[5]

By now you'll have realized that I believe protein to be an essential part of a balanced diet. You should distribute your protein consumption throughout the day. An easy way to do so is to follow the 30-30-30 rule, which means incorporating 30 grams (1 ounce) of protein in each meal so you can draw out all the benefits of a protein-balanced diet. Beyond 30 grams (1 ounce) per meal, your muscles' protein synthesis hits a plateau, making it unnecessary to eat any more. In my job as a nutritionist and dietitian, the main issue I notice with my clients is not a lack in the total amount of protein consumed, but an uneven distribution of protein consumption throughout the day. For example, people who consume the right amount of protein per day, but distributed as 5 grams (0.2 ounce) at breakfast, 15 grams (0.5 ounce) at lunch, and 70 grams (2.5 ounces) at dinner, do not maximize their protein synthesis. The solution is often simply to increase your intake at breakfast and decrease your intake at dinner. This book will help you achieve just that. By adding yogurt to your menu, you will increase the protein content of the dishes you enjoy while decreasing, in most cases, their fat content.

ABOUT FATS

There are four types of lipids (fats). Monounsaturated and polyunsaturated fats–often called the "good" fats–are found in vegetable oils, nuts, seeds, fish, and some fruits like avocados. These fats, and foods that contain them, are associated with diets linked to better health, such as the Mediterranean diet. Trans fats and saturated fats, on the other hand, are largely considered to be the bad guys. They can be found in processed products, red meat, cold cuts, charcuteries . . . and dairy products!

Although dairy products do contain "bad fats," they also provide significant benefits, especially cheese, yogurt, and kefir. Eating dairy products does not increase the risk of cardiovascular events, despite the saturated fats they contain. Yet red meat, which also contains saturated fats, does increase the risk of heart disease. Why is that? One popular theory is that dairy products provide numerous other healthful components, such as calcium, bacteria (probiotics), proteins, bioactive peptides (derived from casein, the protein in milk), and other known dairy fats, such as trans-palmitoleic acid. In fact, Harvard researchers have demonstrated that people who maintain a diet rich in trans-palmitoleic acid had a 60 percent lower risk of developing type-2 diabetes.[6]

WHICH TYPE OF YOGURT SHOULD YOU CHOOSE?

For the past five years, yogurt product offerings have continued to grow. Faced with such a diverse array of products, the customer can easily get lost.

A recent Canadian study concluded that overweight people primarily consume fat-free yogurt, whereas people within normal weight ranges mostly eat yogurts with a higher fat content (2% milk fat and over). An interesting highlight of this study is that the subjects who chose fat-free yogurt did not have a lower-fat diet at day's end, because they would satisfy their craving for fats by eating other high-calorie foods. The researchers also demonstrated that eating any type of yogurt (with or without fat) was associated with lower triglyceride and insulin levels, which promote heart health. The research thus encourages the consumption of yogurt, even higher-fat varieties.[7]

In Europe, although increasing numbers of lighter products are being marketed every year, regular Greek yogurt is especially rich, containing up to 10 grams (0.4 ounces) of fat per 207 mL (7 ounce) serving. This fat content provides an exceptionally rich and creamy texture that satisfies faster than a low-fat variety does. The situation is different in North America, where popular culture has long favored low-fat yogurts. So, for the most part, in North America you'll find a much wider offering of products with a lower fat content (under 2%), even for Greek yogurts.

Because it is high in proteins, good for the heart, and more filling than regular yogurt, I highly recommend eating Greek yogurt–as you've probably guessed. It's up to you to choose your preferred fat content.

SUBSTITUTIONS

Greek yogurt is an excellent substitute for fats used in muffins, cakes, and quick breads (banana, lemon and poppy seed, chocolate, etc.). In cakes, simply make sure to maintain 3 tablespoons (45 mL) of fat (butter, oil, etc.) per cup (250 mL) of flour, and substitute the remaining fat amounts with yogurt. In muffins, you can substitute up to two-thirds of the total fat quantities used in a recipe (butter, oil, etc.) with an equal volume of yogurt.

Here's a handy table that will help you make the right substitutions. These tips will allow you to integrate yogurt into your favorite recipes to increase their protein content and decrease the fat content, thus raising their nutritional value.

ORIGINAL INGREDIENT	GREEK YOGURT SUBSTITUTION		USES
Mayonnaise 1 cup (250 mL)	Regular mayonnaise ¼ cup (60 mL)	Greek yogurt ¾ cup (180 mL)	- Dips - Creamy dressings
	10 times more protein and 75% less fat		
Sour cream 1 cup (250 mL)	Greek yogurt 1 cup (250 mL)		- Potato salad - Fajitas - Oven-baked potatoes - Coleslaw
Ice cream 1 cup (250 mL)	Vanilla Greek yogurt 1 cup (250 mL)		- Frozen cakes - Frozen pies
Crème fraîche 1 cup (250 mL)	Crème fraîche ¼ cup (60 mL)	Greek yogurt ¾ cup (180 mL)	- Soups - Sauces - Mashed potatoes
	3 times more protein		
Cream cheese 1 cup (250 mL)	Cream cheese ½ cup (125 mL)	Greek yogurt ½ cup (125 mL)	- Cheesecake - Cake topping or icing
Cream cheese 1 cup (250 mL)	Greek yogurt 1 cup (250 mL)		- Dips - Spreads
Oil 1 cup (250 mL)	Oil ⅓ cup (80 mL)	Greek yogurt ⅔ cup (160 mL)	- Cakes - Muffins - Scones - Store-bought cake mixes
Butter 1 cup (250 mL)	Butter ½ cup (125 mL)	Greek yogurt ¼ cup (60 mL)	- Cakes - Muffins - Scones - Cookies

THE RECIPES

KEY

♀ ♀ ♀ *Servings*

⊔ *Prep time*

🌡 *Rest or refrigeration time*

❄ *Freezing time*

🧤 *Cooking time*

The Basics

Essential Recipes to Make Yogurt at Home

There are many benefits to making yogurt at home. First, it allows you to make the exact quantity you need. This is handy, for example, if you plan to leave on a trip. You can make only the yogurt you know you'll consume before your departure, eliminating any potential waste. You'll also enjoy a fresh product at all times, although yogurt keeps well in the refrigerator for a relatively long time. Finally, making yogurt at home allows you to be creative and to add fun flavors, fresh fruit, jam, or herbs and spices. In fact, each jar you make could be a different flavor! For example, you could infuse your yogurt with fresh mint and use it in a tzatziki recipe.

The easiest way to make your own yogurt is to use a yogurt maker. This is a small appliance that acts like a steamer to transform milk into yogurt through fermentation. The main advantages of a yogurt maker are that it heats up to and maintains a precise temperature. Some models also have an auto-stop feature, which allows you to start a batch at night and enjoy it the following morning.

Here's a method to make yogurt with a yogurt maker. This method will work with most models, but be sure to read and follow the instructions on your specific machine.

8 servings   *30 minutes*   *4 ½ hours*

1. Bring 4 cups (1 L) milk to a boil.
2. Remove from the heat and let the milk cool down to 108°F to 112°F (42°C to 44°C).
3. In a small bowl, dilute one packet (0.18 ounce/5 g) yogurt starter into a small quantity of the warmed milk. Transfer this mixture back into the rest of the warm milk and whisk to combine.
4. Set fermentation time to 4½ hours, or ferment until it reaches your desired consistency (refer to the manufacturer's manual for more information on fermentation times).
5. Refrigerate to stop the fermentation process. Keep the yogurt refrigerated until ready to enjoy.

WHERE CAN I FIND YOGURT STARTER?

You can find yogurt starter in the refrigerated section of supermarkets or at health food stores. Yogurt starter is necessary to thicken yogurt and give it a creamy consistency. If you don't have or can't find yogurt starter, you can use yogurt itself to act as a starter (just reach for that near-empty yogurt container sitting at the back of your fridge!). You will need ½ cup (125 mL) of yogurt per 4 cups (1 L) of milk. The more starter you use, the firmer and more acidic the resulting yogurt will be.

OTHER TIPS

Swiss, or stirred, yogurt is the most common type of yogurt you can make at home. It has a creamy texture, but the consistency remains fairly runny. To thicken the yogurt, increase the fermentation and refrigeration time. The longer the fermentation and refrigeration times, the firmer the yogurt will be.

Balkan-style yogurt is thicker than stirred yogurt. When you make yogurt at home, it's difficult to replicate the same conditions every time, and any change in humidity or timing will affect the final texture of the product. However, to make yogurt with a thicker consistency, you can add skim milk powder, heavy cream (added to the milk to increase the fat content), gelatin, or agar-agar. You can also strain the yogurt to remove some of its water content. Skyr, an Icelandic fresh cheese product, and Greek yogurt are both strained products, and the straining is what provides these products their iconic rich, thick texture and high protein content. You need to start with 12 cups (3 L) of milk to make these types of yogurts. Use the method described on page 19 to strain yogurt. The longer you strain it, the thicker it will be.

Making Yogurt Without a Yogurt Maker

You can make yogurt at home without buying a yogurt maker (and cluttering up your kitchen cabinets with another appliance!). Here's how:

8 servings   1 hour   4 to 6 hours

INGREDIENTS

4 cups (1 L) milk (preferably ultra-high temperature, which is shelf-stable, or partly skimmed milk)

Sugar, to taste (optional)

Vanilla extract or other natural or artificial flavorings, to taste (optional)

½ cup (125 mL) skim milk powder (optional for thicker yogurt)

½ cup (125 mL) plain yogurt (to act as starter) or 1 packet (0.18 ounce/5 g) yogurt starter

METHOD

1. In a large saucepan, bring the milk to a gentle simmer over low heat. Add the sugar, the vanilla extract or flavorings of your choice, and the skim milk powder, if using.

2. Let the milk simmer until reduced by a third. This step should take about 30 minutes. Note that the more you reduce the milk, the thicker the resulting yogurt will be.

3. Take the milk off the heat and cover the saucepan with a clean dish towel.

4. Let the milk cool to about 110°F (43°C).

5. Add the plain yogurt or yogurt starter and whisk until the mixture is smooth.

6. Strain the mixture to remove the skin that may have formed over the milk during the simmering process. (It is perfectly normal for a skin to form over the milk during cooking. When the milk is simmering, water evaporates and milk proteins coagulate, and both factors contribute to the formation of a skin on the surface of the hot milk.)

7. Pour the warm milk mixture into small glass jars and seal with lids or plastic wrap.

8. Place the jars in a baking dish and fill the dish with warm water. The water should be level with the milk.

9. Carefully transfer the baking dish to a 125°F (50°C) oven and leave in for 15 minutes.

10. Turn the oven off. With the oven door slightly ajar, let the yogurt set for 4 to 6 hours, then drain the baking dish and refrigerate. The yogurt will firm up as it cools. Enjoy your homemade yogurt within 2 weeks.

Making Yogurt Using a Slow Cooker

This unusual slow-cooker method will show you how easy it is to make yogurt at home. Don't be skeptical: it really works! The only tools you need, besides a slow cooker, are a thermometer and a bath towel (and, perhaps, a bit of patience).

16 servings   4 hours, elapsed   5 hours

INGREDIENTS

8 cups (2 L) whole milk (3.25% milk fat)

1/3 cup (80 mL) skim milk powder (optional)

1 cup (250 mL) plain yogurt

METHOD

1. Pour the milk in the slow cooker's removable stoneware container. Whisk in the skim milk powder, if using.

2. Turn on the slow cooker to the low heat setting and cook for 2 hours or until the milk has reached a temperature of 180°F (82°C). Make sure you check the milk temperature regularly.

3. When the milk reaches the right temperature, turn the slow cooker off and let the milk cool, uncovered, until it comes down to 125°F (50°C). This step will take about 2 hours.

4. Once the milk reaches the right temperature, scoop out 1 cup (250 mL), transfer to a small bowl, and whisk in the plain yogurt. Transfer this mixture back into the slow cooker and whisk thoroughly.

5. Cover the slow cooker and wrap a bath towel around it to retain the remaining heat, which will encourage the development of the necessary bacteria.

6. Let the milk rest at room temperature for at least 5 hours. After that period, check whether the yogurt has set; if it has, whisk the mixture again.

7. Transfer the yogurt to airtight containers and keep refrigerated.

Plant-Based Yogurts

The most common type of yogurt is made with cow's milk. However, some people are intolerant to lactose and/or allergic to milk proteins, making it difficult or downright dangerous to consume cow's milk yogurt. If this applies to you, you have likely found that store-bought dairy-free products or yogurts made with plant milks, such as soy milk, serve as handy substitutes.

But did you know that you can make your own dairy-free yogurt at home? Simply replace cow's milk with goat's milk or soy milk at a 1:1 ratio and make yogurt using any of the methods described previously.

Coconut Yogurt

Coconut yogurt is another deliciously creamy, dairy-free option. You can easily make your own coconut yogurt following a few simple steps. First you need an additional ingredient: probiotic capsules, which you can find at drugstores or health food stores. For the best results, look for probiotic capsules that contain the following strains: *Lactobacillus acidophilus*, *Bifidobacterium bifidum*, *Bifidobacterium lactis*, or *Streptococcus thermophilus*.
When using coconut milk, you also need a thickening agent to reach a yogurt-like consistency. I like to use agar-agar, which is a great plant-based alternative to gelatin.

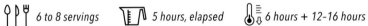 6 to 8 servings   5 hours, elapsed   6 hours + 12–16 hours

INGREDIENTS

Two 14-ounce (398 mL) cans coconut milk

1 teaspoon (5 mL) agar-agar powder

4 capsules probiotics (or an equivalent that provides over 75 billion bacteria) or ¼ cup (60 mL) coconut yogurt

2 tablespoons (30 mL) granulated sugar or maple syrup (optional)

METHOD

1. Pour the coconut milk in a saucepan and whisk to smooth the thicker cream into the watery liquid.

2. Sprinkle 1 teaspoon (5 mL) agar-agar over the coconut milk. Do not mix; let the agar-agar rest for a while.

3. Heat the coconut milk over medium heat until tiny bubbles start to rise to the surface. Whisk and turn the heat down to low. Simmer for 7 to 10 minutes or until the agar-agar is completely dissolved.

4. Remove from the heat and let the milk cool down to 108°F to 112°F (42°C to 44°C).

5. Add the probiotics. To do so, simply open each capsule and transfer only the powder into the warm milk mixture. Whisk vigorously to combine.

6. Incorporate the sugar or maple syrup, if using.

7. Pour the warm milk mixture into small glass jars and seal with lids or plastic wrap.

8. Transfer the jars into a yogurt maker and set the fermentation time to 4½ hours, or ferment until the yogurt reaches your desired consistency (refer to the manufacturer's manual for more information on fermentation times). You can also set the jars on a baking sheet and place them in a turned-off oven with the light on (to provide a faint heat source) for 12 to 16 hours.

9. Place the coconut yogurt jars in the refrigerator for about 6 hours. The yogurt will thicken as it cools. If a thin yellow film forms over the yogurt after cooling, simply spoon it off for a creamier texture or mix it into the yogurt to combine both layers. Coconut yogurt will keep refrigerated for up to 2 weeks.

Yogurt Mayonnaise

I've been mixing mayo with plain yogurt for years now. This allows me to lower the fat content of the mayo I use and to benefit from a higher protein content. I mostly use Greek yogurt, but if I need a sauce that is more liquid, I use a high-fat regular plain yogurt, which is a great alternative. You can go wild by seasoning yogurt mayo with all sorts of flavorings, including spices, herbs, or natural flavors. I like to season mine with curry powder, turmeric, and honey. For variety, I sometimes add a bit of tomato paste or chili sauce.

1 cup   *5 minutes*

INGREDIENTS
¼ cup mayonnaise

¾ cup plain Greek yogurt (regular or high in fat)

Seasonings of your choice

METHOD
1. In an airtight container, mix the mayonnaise and yogurt together.
2. Season to taste. The yogurt mayo will keep refrigerated for a few days.

Strained Greek yogurt

Greek yogurt has an enticing creamy, thick texture. However, some recipes require an even thicker texture, similar to that of cheese spread or mascarpone cheese. During the straining process, part of the yogurt's whey (lactoserum) is removed. The result is a very firm yogurt.

5 minutes   *4 hours*

INGREDIENTS
2 cups plain Greek yogurt

METHOD
1. Line a strainer with cheesecloth (or a clean kitchen towel, piece of paper towel, or coffee filter).
2. Pour the Greek yogurt into the lined strainer. Set the strainer over a bowl and refrigerate for at least 4 hours. The longer you let the yogurt strain, the thicker it will be.
3. Transfer the strained yogurt to an airtight container and refrigerate for up to a week.

My Yogurt Bar

Fresh fruit, diced
(I used kiwifruits and pomegranate seeds)

Kumquat marmalade

Cranberry jam

[ON THE SWEET SIDE]

Making and Giving Yogurt

Always at a loss when it comes to finding a host or hostess gift idea when you're invited to dinner? Small jars of homemade yogurt along with creative flavorings will delight your hosts the morning after. Homemade yogurt can also be eaten as a dessert, depending on the garnishes you choose. Don't hesitate to use inspiration from this book to make your own jarred creations! You could, for example, add tapioca (bubble-tea-style, p. 45) or salted caramel (p. 169), or you could make a delicious panna cotta (p. 165).

Organizing a special event, a baby shower, or a dinner party? Set up a yogurt bar like the one shown below; your guests will love it! Serve individual portions of yogurt in small glass jars and set garnishes along the table so each guest can choose their own. Consider offering both sweet and savory options.

Caramelized rosemary pecans

Tzatziki mix
(mint, cucumber, garlic, and lime juice)

Pesto and walnuts

[ON THE SAVOURY SIDE]

1
Breakfast

Chia and Kiwi Pudding with Green Grape Sauce

I discovered green grape sauce at a restaurant that served it with grilled scallops. I immediately fell in love with the sauce's taste, which is both sweet and subtle. I soon made it at home, and it was a revelation. With this sauce, you won't ever need to add sugar or syrup over breakfast dishes again! In this recipe, the sauce beautifully enhances the flavor of kiwifruits while adding a sweet touch. It's an incredibly fresh-tasting dish!

 *2 servings*　　*10 minutes*　　*1 hour (or overnight)*

INGREDIENTS

1 cup (250 mL) plain Greek yogurt

¼ cup (60 mL) whole white chia seeds

2 tablespoons (30 mL) honey

2 kiwifruits, diced

30 green grapes

mint leaves, for garnish

METHOD

1. In a bowl, combine the yogurt and chia seeds.
2. Divide the honey between two small serving jars (1 tablespoon/15 mL per jar).
3. Divide the yogurt between the jars.
4. Add the diced kiwifruits.
5. Fill a large pot with water and bring to a boil. Blanch the green grapes for about 1 minute, then rinse under cold water.
6. Peel the grapes.
7. Using a food processor, process the grapes until you reach a smooth consistency.
8. Divide the green grape sauce between the jars, pouring it over the kiwifruit layer.
9. Refrigerate for 1 hour (or overnight) and garnish with mint just before serving.

Hubert's Tip: *Have any sauce left over? Freeze it for future use, or serve it as a granita.*

Nutritional value (per serving)
Calories: 366 Total fat: 9.7 g Saturated fats: 2.1 g Cholesterol: 11 mg
Sodium: 55 mg Carbohydrates: 58 g Fibers: 13 g Protein: 16 g

Overnight Oats

This is the perfect breakfast for rushed mornings. You can take it with you and eat it on public transit or enjoy it when you get to work or school. I love that you can flavor it so many different ways. And it's really easy, too: all you need to do is top the dry oats with a serving of plain or flavored Greek yogurt, and some frozen fruit (if you're using fresh fruit, you can add it the morning of!). My favorite fruit topping for this is fresh mango, which I cut into cubes and drop over my yogurt and oats concoction. You could always stir in the fruit, but the effort is not really required.

2 servings   *5 minutes*   *Overnight*

INGREDIENTS

1 cup (250 mL) rolled oats

1⅓ cups (320 mL) plain Greek yogurt

½ cup (125 mL) almond milk

2 tablespoons (30 mL) honey or maple syrup

½ teaspoon (2.5 mL) ground cardamom

Ground nutmeg, to taste

1 mango, or frozen or fresh fruit of your choice

METHOD

1. Divide the rolled oats between two glass jars.
2. In a bowl, combine the yogurt, almond milk, honey, cardamom, and nutmeg.
3. Pour the yogurt mixture over the oats.
4. Add the frozen fruit of your choice. If you're using fresh fruit, wait to add it in the morning.
5. Seal the jars and refrigerate overnight.

Hubert's Tip: *If you're pressed for time or don't have fresh fruit at home, use canned fruit instead. You can also substitute unsweetened fruit compote.*

Nutritional value (per serving)
Calories: 425   Total fat: 7.1 g   Saturated fats: 2.8 g   Cholesterol: 15 mg
Sodium: 112 mg   Carbohydrates: 70 g   Fibers: 7 g   Protein: 23 g

Fruits en Papillote

I really enjoy brunches and long breakfasts with the family. Less formal than dinners, such meals allow me to share good times without having a drink! This dish is perfect for a brunch spread. Just wrap lots of fruit into a paper parcel (also called a "papillote") and set it in the middle of the table so everyone can garnish their own bowl of Greek yogurt with their favorite fruit. The taste is completely different from a classic fresh fruit topping, and it's a unique way to enjoy fruit.

 4 servings   15 minutes   35 minutes

INGREDIENTS

For the papillote

2 peaches, diced

2 pears, diced

1 cup (250 mL) halved strawberries

1 cup (250 mL) blackberries

2 tablespoons (30 mL) granulated sugar

2 tablespoons (30 mL) unsweetened apple juice

½ teaspoon (2.5 mL) lime zest

2 teaspoons (10 mL) Grand Marnier (or other citrus fruit liqueur)

To serve

2 cups (500 mL) plain Greek yogurt

2 tablespoons (30 mL) slivered almonds

METHOD

1. Preheat the oven to 400°F (200°C).
2. In a large bowl, mix the fruits, sugar, apple juice, lime zest, and Grand Marnier.
3. Line a baking sheet with two sheets of parchment paper measuring 12 × 16 inches (30 × 40 cm). Transfer the fruit mixture to the center of the parchment paper, then gather all sides together to form a bundle. Twist the top of the bundle to seal it.
4. Bake for 35 minutes.
5. Set the baked papillote in the middle of the table, along with plain Greek yogurt and slivered almonds, so every guest can help themselves.

Nutritional value (for ¼ of the fruit + ½ cup Greek yogurt)
Calories: 271   Total fat: 6.8 g   Saturated fats: 1.8 g   Cholesterol: 11 mg
Sodium: 49 mg   Carbohydrates: 38 g   Fibers: 7 g   Protein: 15 g

Baked Oatmeal

Sometimes you have to be creative in the kitchen. When I make oatmeal, I like to double or even triple quantities so I have some leftovers that I can use in other recipes. Baked oatmeal looks like a small muffin made with cooked oatmeal; just add whatever flavors you have a craving for. In this recipe, I added dried fruit while the oatmeal was cooking.

 12 mini-muffins   30 minutes   45 minutes

INGREDIENTS

3 cups (750 mL) water

1⅓ cups (320 mL) rolled oats

Pinch of salt

½ cup (125 mL) dried or freeze-dried fruits (mango, pineapple, raisins, or banana), chopped then measured

1 egg

⅓ cup (80 mL) vanilla Greek yogurt

Dried coconut flakes (optional)

METHOD

1. Preheat the oven to 375°F (190°C).
2. Pour the water into a saucepan. Add the rolled oats, salt, and fruits. Cook the oats for 20 minutes or until they reach your desired consistency.
3. Transfer to a large bowl and let cool for 5 minutes.
4. Mix in the egg and Greek yogurt.
5. Grease a 12-cup mini-muffin pan (or use paper liners). Fill each cup with some of the oat mixture.
6. Sprinkle with dried coconut flakes, if using.
7. Bake for 25 minutes.

Hubert's Tip: *Freeze the muffins so you'll always have some on hand. One muffin is the perfect addition to a balanced breakfast.*

Nutritional value (per mini-muffin)
Calories: 74   Total fat: 1.6 g   Saturated fats: 0.7 g   Cholesterol: 17 mg
Sodium: 23 mg   Carbohydrates: 13 g   Fibers: 2 g   Protein: 3 g

Yogurt Pancakes

Who doesn't love crepes and pancakes? When I was a kid, my mom would make me crepes on Saturday mornings as a reward for good school grades. I loved her crepes, and I always sprinkled a bit of brown sugar and drizzled some maple syrup over top. Years later, I discovered pancakes. Here's my favorite protein-packed recipe. You can transform this recipe into thin and crispy crepes by thinning the batter with more unsweetened almond milk.

 12 pancakes   *5 minutes*   *10 minutes*

INGREDIENTS

1 cup (250 mL) plain Greek yogurt

1 cup (250 mL) all-purpose flour

¾ cup (180 mL) unsweetened almond milk

2 tablespoons (30 mL) granulated sugar

½ teaspoon (2.5 mL) baking soda

½ teaspoon (2.5 mL) salt

1 egg

1 teaspoon (5 mL) vanilla extract

Pinch of ground cinnamon or nutmeg (optional)

METHOD

1. In a large mixing bowl, combine the Greek yogurt, flour, almond milk, sugar, baking soda, and salt.

2. In a second mixing bowl, whisk the egg and add the vanilla extract and cinnamon or nutmeg, if using.

3. Combine the egg mixture into the yogurt mixture. Do not overmix.

4. Pour about ¼ cup (60 mL) batter into an oiled crepe pan or nonstick skillet. Cook over medium heat for 25 to 30 seconds, then flip the pancake. Cook on the second side for 30 seconds. Transfer the cooked pancake to a serving plate. Repeat for the remaining batter, adding more oil to the skillet if needed.

5. Serve the pancakes with maple syrup.

Hubert's Tip: *To increase the recipe's protein and healthy fat content, add chopped walnuts, pecans, or pistachios to the pancake batter. As a variation, add berries to the mix.*

Nutritional value (for 3 pancakes)
Calories: 219 Total fat: 3.9 g Saturated fats: 1.3 g Cholesterol: 54 mg
Sodium: 265 mg Carbohydrates: 34 g Fibers: 2 g Protein: 12 g

Wafflewich

I've loved waffles for as long as I can remember. In Québec, we often enjoy waffles drizzled with maple syrup and sprinkled with cinnamon. In this recipe, I'm reimagining the classic recipe by turning it savory. The waffles replace classic sandwich bread slices, creating a "wafflewich"! Just add a lean protein and the vegetables of your choice.

 8 waffles   10 minutes   30 minutes   5 minutes (refer to the waffle iron manufacturer's instructions)

INGREDIENTS

1¾ cups (425 mL) all-purpose flour

1 packet (8 mL) instant dry yeast

½ teaspoon (2.5 mL) salt

2 eggs

¼ cup (60 mL) butter, melted

¼ cup (60 mL) plain Greek yogurt

1⅔ cups (400 mL) milk

½ cup (125 mL) shredded light cheddar

METHOD

1. In a large bowl, combine the flour, instant dry yeast, and salt.

2. Mix in the eggs, melted butter, and yogurt, then incorporate the milk. Beat until you reach a smooth consistency.

3. Stir in the cheese.

4. Cover the mixing bowl with a damp towel and let the batter rest for 30 minutes.

5. Oil the plates of the waffle iron and heat as per the manufacturer's instructions, then pour on some batter to cover the whole surface (but be careful not to overfill).

6. Cook each waffle for about 5 minutes. The cooking time will vary depending on the size of the waffles you make and the type of waffle iron you use.

7. Once the waffles are cooked and have cooled slightly, pair two of them with your desired spreads and sandwich fillings, and enjoy!

Hubert's Tip: *I often use yogurt mayonnaise (p. 19) as a base to make a garlic and chive spread. You can also simply use equal parts light cream cheese and strained yogurt and add ½ tablespoon (7.5 mL) minced garlic and chopped chives to taste.*

Nutritional value (for 2 waffles)
Calories: 524   Total fat: 21 g   Saturated fats: 11.4 g   Cholesterol: 142 mg
Sodium: 496 mg   Carbohydrates: 60 g   Fibers: 2 g   Protein: 22 g

Oats-Filled Baked Apples

I've long had the habit of dicing an apple and adding it to my morning oats. Here I do the reverse: I stuff the cooked oats into the apple. The slowly baking apples and spices will fill your kitchen with a truly divine aroma.

4 servings   *15 minutes*   *40 minutes*

INGREDIENTS

4 apples

½ cup (125 mL) cooked oats

½ cup (125 mL) vanilla Greek yogurt

¼ cup (60 mL) dried cranberries

12 walnut halves

½ cup (125 mL) pistachios

½ teaspoon (2.5 mL) freshly grated nutmeg

½ teaspoon (2.5 mL) ground cinnamon

¾ cup (180 mL) apple juice

3 tablespoons (45 mL) maple syrup or brown sugar

METHOD

1. Preheat the oven to 350°F (180°C).
2. Cut off the base of the apples so they are stable and stand up straight.
3. Using a melon baller, remove the core of each apple, leaving about ½ inch (1 cm) of flesh at the bottom.
4. In a mixing bowl, combine the cooked oats, yogurt, dried cranberries, walnuts, pistachios, nutmeg, and cinnamon.
5. Fill each apple cavity with some of the oat mixture.
6. Place the filled apples in a baking pan.
7. Pour the apple juice around the apples, and drizzle the maple syrup (or sprinkle the brown sugar) over the top of each apple.
8. Bake for 40 minutes or until the apples are tender.

Hubert's Tip: *Swap oats for hulled barley or quinoa, or even a combination of the three grains.*

Nutritional value (per serving)
Calories: 276   Total fat: 6.6 g   Saturated fats: 1 g   Cholesterol: 3 mg
Sodium: 16 mg   Carbohydrates: 53 g   Fibers: 5 g   Protein: 6 g

Milkshake

Long considered a dessert, milkshakes, in my opinion, should have their spot at breakfast, too. You simply need to swap a few ingredients to create a harmony of flavors that will delight your taste buds. In this recipe, I use Greek yogurt as a substitute for ice cream. The addition of colorful sprinkles that melt and leave a rainbow trail in the glass are a nod to the ice cream parlors of my youth.

2 servings   *5 minutes*

INGREDIENTS

1 frozen banana

1 cup (250 mL) unsweetened almond milk

2 tablespoons (30 mL) almond butter

¾ cup (180 mL) plain Greek yogurt

1 tablespoon (15 mL) honey

Chopped walnuts (optional)

Ice cream sprinkles or fresh fruit, for garnish (optional)

METHOD

1. Take the banana out of the freezer and run it under hot water for a few seconds. Cut it into chunks.

2. In a blender, add the banana chunks, almond milk, almond butter, yogurt, and honey. If using walnuts, add them too.

3. Blend until the milkshake is smooth.

4. Divide between two tall glasses and garnish with sprinkles or fresh fruits.

Hubert's Tip: *You can freeze bananas, peeled or not. If you freeze a banana with the peel on, the peel will turn black but the flesh will remain perfectly edible. Frozen unpeeled bananas will keep for at least 2 months in the freezer, whereas peeled bananas will keep for up to 4 months.*

Nutritional value (per serving)
Calories: 263   Total fat: 12.8 g   Saturated fats: 2 g   Cholesterol: 8 mg
Sodium: 115 mg   Carbohydrates: 29 g   Fibers: 3 g   Protein: 12 g

Mediterranean Burritos

Mornings can sometimes get incredibly hectic. I'm sure you have no time to cook a fussy breakfast for the whole family on a weekday, especially if you also need to prepare lunches. Fifteen minutes are all you need to concoct this healthy breakfast wrap. You can easily double the recipe and freeze the assembled burritos to make for an even faster breakfast later in the week.

 2 servings 10 minutes 5 minutes

INGREDIENTS

2 eggs

2 egg whites

½ cup (125 mL) plain Greek yogurt

½ teaspoon (2.5 mL) ground cumin

Salt and pepper, to taste

½ cup (125 mL) tomato salsa (or diced tomato)

½ avocado, sliced

Two 6-inch (15 cm) spinach flour tortillas

1 cup (250 mL) canned black beans, drained and rinsed

METHOD

1. In a mixing bowl, whisk the eggs, egg whites, Greek yogurt, cumin, salt, and pepper together.

2. Pour the mixture into a nonstick skillet and cook for about 5 minutes over medium-low heat. Gently scrape the bottom of the skillet to create soft egg lumps.

3. Mix in the salsa.

4. Divide the avocado slices between the tortillas. Top with the black beans, then the egg mixture.

5. Roll the tortillas tightly, cut in halves, and serve.

Hubert's Tip: *Adding Greek yogurt to the egg and black bean burrito mixture increases the protein value of the dish. The ideal protein content of every meal, including breakfast, is 20 to 30 grams (0.7 to 1 ounce).*

Nutritional value (per burrito)
Calories: 354 Total fat: 12.8 g Saturated fats: 3.2 g Cholesterol: 198 mg
Sodium: 156 mg Carbohydrates: 36 g Fibers: 10 g Protein: 25 g

Healthy Exotic Bowl with Dragon Fruit and Lychee

I've always been fascinated by color. I was a bit of an artist as a kid, and I loved to draw. The colors on our plates are just as important as the colors that surround us; they set the tone and grab our attention. We're all attracted by what's colorful, which is why you'll love this vibrant exotic breakfast bowl, especially on cloudier days. The combination of beets and grapefruit will surprise you! I let my creativity run free to harmonize the colors in this bowl; feel free to do the same at home.

2 servings   *10 minutes*

INGREDIENTS

2 cups (500 mL) plain Greek yogurt

1 cooked beet, diced

½ cup (125 mL) fresh or frozen raspberries

¼ cup (60 mL) grapefruit juice

2 kiwifruits, diced

4 lychees

½ mango

½ pitahaya (dragon fruit)

2 tablespoons (30 mL) goji berries

2 tablespoons (30 mL) shelled unsalted pistachios

2 tablespoons (30 mL) unsalted pumpkin seeds

METHOD

1. In a food processor, combine the Greek yogurt, beet, raspberries, and grapefruit juice, and process until the mixture is smooth.

2. Divide between two bowls, then top with the rest of the fruit, pistachios, and pumpkin seeds.

Nutritional value (per serving)
Calories: 368   Total fat: 10.3 g   Saturated fats: 3.4 g   Cholesterol: 22 mg
Sodium: 117 mg   Carbohydrates: 45 g   Fibers: 9 g   Protein: 27 g

Tapioca Velouté

Inspired by the black pearls of tapioca I saw in bubble tea, I went to an Asian grocery store to find the ingredients to make some at home. I stumbled upon large white tapioca pearls, which inspired me to create this whimsical recipe.

2 servings   25 minutes   15 minutes

INGREDIENTS

For the tapioca

4 cups (1 L) water

1 cup (250 mL) large white tapioca pearls

1½ cups (375 mL) plain Greek yogurt

¾ cup (180 mL) almond milk

1 vanilla pod, or 1 teaspoon (5 mL) vanilla extract

For the raspberry coulis

¼ cup (60 mL) frozen raspberries

2 tablespoons (30 mL) granulated sugar

METHOD

For the tapioca

1. In a large pot, bring the water to a boil. Add the tapioca pearls and cook for 15 minutes.
2. Turn off the heat and let rest for 5 minutes.
3. Drain the tapioca pearls, then rinse them thoroughly under cold water. Set aside.
4. In a large mixing bowl, combine the yogurt, almond milk, and vanilla seeds. Divide between two serving bowls, and add the tapioca pearls.

For the raspberry coulis

5. In a nonstick skillet, cook the raspberries over medium heat. Add the sugar and stir continuously until the mixture reaches a smooth and sauce-like texture.
6. Drizzle a bit of the raspberry coulis over the tapioca and serve.

Hubert's Tip: *The consistency of the tapioca pearls depends on the cooking time. The pearls shouldn't be too soft or too firm. You can also use regular tapioca, but make sure to read the manufacturer's instructions to prepare it properly.*

Nutritional value (per serving)
Calories: 476 Total fat: 12.5 g Saturated fats: 7.4 g Cholesterol: 35 mg
Sodium: 176 mg Carbohydrates: 80 g Fibers: 3 g Protein: 9 g

Sharp Cheddar Macaroni

For most people, breakfast equals bread. But pasta is a starch, too, so why not use it as a sidekick to eggs? This breakfast mac and cheese is a perfect side to a Sunday brunch omelette, just omit the poached egg.

4 servings — *25 minutes* — *15 minutes*

INGREDIENTS

For the macaroni

2 cups (500 mL) dry macaroni

3 tablespoons (45 mL) unsalted butter

3 tablespoons (45 mL) all-purpose flour

1 cup (250 mL) plain yogurt (1% or 2% milk fat)

1 cup (250 mL) shredded Gouda

1 cup (250 mL) shredded sharp cheddar, divided

1 tablespoon (15 mL) Dijon mustard

1 cup (250 mL) chopped kale

1 teaspoon (5 mL) garlic powder

Salt and pepper, to taste

For the poached eggs

4 eggs

2 tablespoons (30 mL) white vinegar

Hubert's Tip: *If you have some firm tofu in the refrigerator, grate it and sprinkle it over the macaroni before broiling it. This handy tip works with any au gratin recipe, allowing you to decrease the amount of cheese you use and, consequently, the fat content of the dish.*

METHOD

1. Cook the macaroni according to the manufacturer's instructions. Reserve 1 cup (250 mL) of the pasta cooking water, then drain the pasta. Set aside.

2. While the macaroni cooks, poach your eggs. Add the vinegar to a pan of simmering water, then create a gentle whirlpool to help the egg white wrap around the yolk. Slowly tip the egg into the water, and cook for 3 minutes. Remove the egg with a slotted spoon and set it on a plate lined with a paper towel.

3. Put the macaroni pot back over medium-low heat, and add the butter to melt it. Add the flour and cook, stirring, for 2 minutes.

4. Add the yogurt and whisk to combine. Gradually add the Gouda and half of the cheddar, alternating with some of the reserved pasta cooking water, and whisk until the sauce is creamy and smooth. Mix in the Dijon mustard, kale, and garlic powder.

5. Add the cooked pasta to the cheese sauce and mix to combine. Season to taste.

6. Transfer the macaroni to four ovenproof ramekins and sprinkle with the remaining cheddar.

7. Set the ramekins on a baking sheet and place on the oven's center rack. Broil for a few minutes or until the cheese is golden and bubbly. Top each ramekin with a poached egg, and serve.

Nutritional value (per serving)
Calories: 600 Total fat: 35.1 g Saturated fats: 20 g Cholesterol: 288 mg
Sodium: 611 mg Carbohydrates: 40 g Fibers: 2 g Protein: 31 g

Eggs Benedict with Lighter Hollandaise Sauce

I have the bad habit of always ordering the same dishes at restaurants. At brunch, if eggs Benedict is on the menu, I will inevitably fall for it. But it's a very rich dish, so I've developed my own lighter version of the classic hollandaise sauce. This allows me to make my favorite brunch dish at home as often as I have a craving for it, guilt free!

 4 servings   10 to 15 minutes   5 to 6 minutes

INGREDIENTS

3 tablespoons (45 mL) butter, divided

2 tablespoons (30 mL) all-purpose flour

1 tablespoon (15 mL) white wine

¾ cup (180 mL) milk

Pepper, to taste

2 egg yolks

¼ cup (60 mL) plain yogurt

A few drops of lemon juice

4 toasted whole wheat English muffins

8 poached eggs

METHOD

1. Melt half the butter in a saucepan. Whisk in the flour and the wine, and cook about 1 minute over medium heat.

2. Add the milk and cook, stirring, about 5 minutes. Season with pepper to taste.

3. In a small bowl, whisk the egg yolks, then whisk in a bit of the hot sauce.

4. Transfer the egg yolks to the sauce, and cook for 2 minutes, while whisking, until the sauce thickens. Remove from the heat.

5. Melt the remaining butter and whisk it, along with the yogurt and lemon juice, into the sauce.

6. Top each toasted English muffin with a poached egg and a quarter of the hollandaise sauce.

Hubert's Tip: *I like to serve eggs Benedict over toasted whole wheat English muffins. I also usually add a protein, such as sausage meat, Black Forest ham, shredded confit duck meat, or smoked salmon.*

Nutritional value (per serving of English muffin, eggs and sauce)
Calories: 429   Total fat: 23.5 g   Saturated fats: 9.9 g   Cholesterol: 488 mg
Sodium: 473 mg   Carbohydrates: 35 g   Fibers: 5 g   Protein: 22 g

Frozen Smoothie Cubes

What is the major drawback of making smoothies in the morning? The noise! The noise! To avoid waking everyone up by turning on the blender in the early morning, I thought up a genius solution: make the smoothie ahead of time and freeze it in ice cube trays. Simply drop a few cubes in a glass before you go to bed, and your smoothie will be ready when you wake up. Make sure to cycle through flavors to please all the smoothie lovers in your family. It's a sure hit!

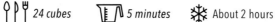 24 cubes   5 minutes   About 2 hours

INGREDIENTS

1½ cups (375 mL) plain or vanilla Greek yogurt, divided

Fresh or frozen fruits and vegetables, to taste

Apple juice, to taste

METHOD

1. Scoop 1 tablespoon (15 mL) Greek yogurt into each cavity of two ice trays. Freeze for about 1 hour.

2. Meanwhile, blend together fruits and vegetables of a single color to make a puree. If the puree is too thick, add some apple juice. The texture must be smooth but not too loose.

3. Divide the puree between the ice cube tray cavities, pouring it over the frozen yogurt. Freeze until solid.

4. When the smoothie cubes are solid, unmold and store in airtight freezer bags, labeling each bag with the flavors used.

5. At night, fill a glass with smoothie cubes and let it rest overnight in the refrigerator. Enjoy the next morning!

Hubert's Tip: *To save time, you can also freeze whole cubes of yogurt and whole cubes of fruit and vegetable puree separately. Simply combine the flavors of your choice and thaw overnight, as instructed.*

Nutritional value
Nutritional values vary according to the fruits and vegetables you choose and the number of cubes you use to make a smoothie.

2
Lunch

Cold Cucumber, Yogurt, and Dill Soup

Cucumber is frequently featured in lunch bags and on veggie platters. Its fresh taste also makes it a great addition to many recipes. This soup is the perfect dish to serve on a hot summer day. A few sprigs of dill enhance the flavors of this bright cold soup.

4 servings 10 minutes 1 hour

INGREDIENTS

3 cups (750 mL) peeled, cored, and cubed cucumber

1 clove garlic

1 cup (250 mL) vegetable broth

¾ cup (180 mL) plain Greek yogurt

¼ cup (60 mL) crème fraîche

Fresh dill, to taste

Salt and pepper, to taste

For garnish

Fresh dill

Feta cheese, crumbled

Thin cucumber slices

METHOD

1. In a blender, add the cucumber, garlic, vegetable broth, yogurt, and crème fraîche. Blend until the soup is smooth and creamy.

2. Add dill and season to taste. Refrigerate for 1 hour.

3. To serve, garnish each portion with fresh dill, feta cheese, and cucumber slices.

Nutritional value (per serving)
Calories: 113 Total fat: 6.8 g Saturated fats: 3.9 g Cholesterol: 24 mg
Sodium: 235 mg Carbohydrates: 8 g Fibers: 1 g Protein: 6 g

Lentil Patties

This recipe is inspired by falafel—vegetarian balls or patties that are usually made from chickpeas. My version features similar ingredients, but the use of lentils as a substitute for chickpeas gives the patties a sturdier, almost meaty taste, which is why I like to serve them as I would burgers. Topping a lentil patty with sautéed mushrooms, kale leaves, and a curried mayo (p. 19) results in a sandwich that is guaranteed to please everyone, even serious meat lovers.

20 patties (5 servings)   *15 minutes*   *10 minutes*

INGREDIENTS

1 tablespoon (15 mL) butter

1 small onion, chopped

2 cloves garlic, chopped

1 zucchini, grated

2 bay leaves

2 tablespoons (30 mL) Dijon mustard

1 tablespoon (15 mL) honey or maple syrup

Two 19-ounce (540 mL) cans lentils, drained and rinsed

2 eggs

½ cup (125 mL) grated Parmesan cheese

1⅓ cups (320 mL) bread crumbs

⅓ cup (80 mL) Greek yogurt, strained (see instructions on p. 19)

½ teaspoon (2.5 mL) cayenne pepper

½ teaspoon (2.5 mL) red pepper flakes

Salt and pepper, to taste

METHOD

1. In a nonstick skillet, melt the butter and sauté the onion and garlic. Add the zucchini and bay leaves, and cook for 2 minutes. Remove the bay leaves.

2. Transfer the mixture to a food processor, then add all the remaining ingredients. Process until the ingredients are combined and you reach a texture that resembles ground meat.

3. Create twenty 2-inch (5 cm) patties. If the mixture is too sticky, add more bread crumbs.

4. In a lightly oiled nonstick skillet, cook the patties over medium-high heat.

5. Serve in slider buns, seasoned with curry yogurt mayonnaise (p. 19).

Hubert's Tip: *You can freeze the cooked lentil patties for up to 3 months. As an alternative, serve them with curly lettuce and tomato slices.*

Nutritional value (for 4 patties)
Calories: 502   Total fat: 8.9 g   Saturated fats: 3.3 g   Cholesterol: 88 mg
Sodium: 595 mg   Carbohydrates: 76 g   Fibers: 11 g   Protein: 31 g

Soft-Boiled Eggs and Green Pea Salad

Let's be honest: green peas don't always make a good impression. Their bad rap may be due to the fact that they are rarely eaten fresh, but rather typically poured from a can or thawed from the freezer. Yet this green vegetable has countless good qualities: it's cheap, delicious, and rich in fiber, vitamin C, and vitamin K. This recipe is one of my favorite ways to eat green peas because it's extremely simple, yet rich in taste.

 2 servings   20 minutes   5 minutes

INGREDIENTS

1 tablespoon (15 mL) butter

2 shallots, chopped

4 cloves garlic, finely minced

3 cups (750 mL) frozen green peas, thawed

⅓ cup (80 mL) plain Greek yogurt

⅓ cup (80 mL) cream (15% milk fat)

2 tablespoons (30 mL) rice vinegar

Salt

White vinegar

4 eggs

Fresh mint, to taste

Microgreens, to taste

Salt and pepper, to taste

Hubert's Tip: *To neatly pack this recipe in a lunch box, make hard-boiled eggs instead.*

METHOD

1. In a nonstick skillet, melt the butter over medium heat, and sauté the shallots. Mix in the garlic and remove from heat.

2. Transfer the cooked shallot mixture to a large mixing bowl, and mix in the green peas. Add the yogurt, cream, and rice vinegar, and stir to combine. Divide the salad between two serving plates and set aside.

3. In a saucepan, bring some water to a boil, then add a pinch of salt and a dash of white vinegar. The volume of water must cover the eggs completely.

4. When the water boils, gently drop the eggs into the saucepan. To get a perfect soft-boiled egg, cook for a maximum of 6 minutes.

5. Rinse the eggs under cold water, then peel. To make this easy, gently roll the eggs on a hard surface to crack the shells, then peel the eggs under a trickle of cold water, so no bits of shell remain.

6. Cut the soft-boiled eggs in half, and set over servings of the green pea salad.

7. Garnish with fresh mint and microgreens. Season to taste.

Nutritional value (per serving)
Calories: 461   Total fat: 18.7 g   Saturated fats: 7.8 g   Cholesterol: 410 mg
Sodium: 180 mg   Carbohydrates: 43 g   Fibers: 12.5 g   Protein: 30.7 g

Cauliflower Cream

Cauliflower has a subtle taste, which makes it very versatile. You can add it to soups, pizzas, or couscous. You can also "hide" it as a substitute for many ingredients, such as in my coquilles Saint-Jacques recipe (p. 98), where I combine it with mashed potatoes. In this recipe, cauliflower transforms into a heavenly creamy soup. It's the star of the show!

 6 servings   10 minutes   35 minutes

INGREDIENTS

2 tablespoons (30 mL) extra virgin olive oil

1 onion, finely chopped

1 teaspoon (5 mL) yellow curry paste

1 head cauliflower, cut into florets

4 cups (1 L) vegetable broth

One 19-ounce (540 mL) can lentils, drained and rinsed

Turmeric (optional)

1 cup (250 mL) plain, high-fat Greek yogurt

Pinch of salt

A few drops of Tabasco sauce

For garnish

6 tablespoons (90 mL) plain, high-fat Greek yogurt, divided

Lemon thyme

Salt and pepper, to taste

Croutons

METHOD

1. In a large pot, heat the olive oil and sauté the onion.

2. Add the curry paste and cook, stirring, for 5 minutes, until the onion is translucent.

3. Add the cauliflower florets and vegetable broth. Cover and cook over medium-low heat for about 30 minutes.

4. Add the lentils 5 minutes before the end of the cooking time.

5. Use a blender or a hand blender to process the soup to a smooth and creamy consistency. To give the soup a light yellow tinge, add a bit of turmeric.

6. Whisk in the yogurt, then season with salt and Tabasco sauce.

7. Serve topped with a spoonful of yogurt, fresh lemon thyme, and croutons.

Hubert's Tip: *You can refrigerate or freeze the soup before adding the yogurt. Simply make sure to let it cool completely, then store it in an airtight container. It will keep for up to 2 days in the refrigerator and for up to 4 months in the freezer.*

Nutritional value (per serving)
Calories: 275   Total fat: 9.1 g   Saturated fats: 2.7 g   Cholesterol: 10 mg
Sodium: 659 mg   Carbohydrates: 37 g   Fibers: 7 g   Protein: 14 g

Snow Crab Devilled Eggs

Devilled eggs are popular at dinner parties because they're easy to make. My version is simple but refined thanks to the addition of snow crab meat. The result is simply sublime!

12 devilled eggs   *30 minutes*   *10 minutes*

INGREDIENTS

12 eggs

¼ cup (60 mL) yogurt mayonnaise (p. 19)

Green onions, finely chopped, to taste

5 ounces (150 g) snow crab meat

Salt and pepper, to taste

Sesame seeds, for garnish

Green onion, for garnish

METHOD

1. Place the eggs in a saucepan and cover with cold water. Cover the saucepan and bring to a rolling boil.

2. Remove from the heat and let the eggs rest in the hot water for 20 minutes.

3. Rinse the eggs under cold water, then peel them. To make this easy, gently roll the eggs on a hard surface to crack the shells, then peel the eggs under a trickle of cold water so no bits of shell remain.

4. Cut off the pointy end of each egg, leaving the rest intact. Finely chop the removed hard-boiled egg whites.

5. Using a melon baller, remove the egg yolks.

6. In a bowl, combine the yogurt mayonnaise, green onions, chopped egg whites, and scooped-out egg yolks.

7. Fold in the snow crab meat.

8. Divide the filling among the 12 hard-boiled eggs.

9. Season to taste, and sprinkle with sesame seeds and green onion.

Nutritional value (for 2 devilled eggs)
Calories: 157   Total fat: 10 g   Saturated fats: 2.5 g   Cholesterol: 256 mg
Sodium: 310 mg   Carbohydrates: 2 g   Fibers: 0 g   Protein: 16 g

Green Falafel

I love broccoli in all its forms, and for good reason: it's one of the most nutritious dark green vegetables. When I buy a head of broccoli, I make sure there's no waste. I eat the florets raw with a dip or steamed as a side dish, and I grate the stalk to add it to many recipes, such as coleslaws and salads. This recipe also makes clever use of grated broccoli stalks. The falafel balls are baked and become just as crispy as if they were fried–but they remain much leaner. Keep in mind that you should start this recipe the day before you want to enjoy it.

20 falafel balls (4 servings) · 25 minutes · 24 hours · 20 minutes

INGREDIENTS

1⅓ cups (320 mL) dried chickpeas

1⅓ cups (320 mL) dried lima beans

1 cup (250 mL) grated broccoli stalk

1 shallot

1 bunch flat-leaf parsley

A few fresh cilantro leaves

1 tablespoon (15 mL) ground cumin

¼ cup (60 mL) panko bread crumbs

¼ cup (60 mL) chopped shelled pistachios

1½ cups (375 mL) Greek yogurt, strained (see instructions on p. 19)

METHOD

1. In a large bowl filled with cold water, soak the chickpeas and lima beans for 24 hours. Keep the bowl refrigerated while the pulses soak.

2. The next day, preheat the oven to 375°F (190°C).

3. Drain the pulses, then dry them thoroughly with paper towels.

4. Process the chickpeas, lima beans, broccoli stalk, shallot, parsley, cilantro, cumin, panko bread crumbs, pistachios, and yogurt in a food processor.

5. Shape the mixture into 20 ping-pong-sized balls, and place them on a parchment-lined baking sheet. If the mixture is too sticky, add more panko bread crumbs.

6. Bake the falafel about 20 minutes, turning them every 5 minutes so they brown on all sides evenly.

Hubert's Tip: *You can use canned pulses, but remember that canned pulses are cooked and contain a great deal of water, so definitely don't try to fry these. I like to serve the falafel over a green salad.*

Nutritional value (for 5 falafel)
Calories: 226 Total fat: 5.8 g Saturated fats: 1 g Cholesterol: 2 mg
Sodium: 78 mg Carbohydrates: 233 g Fibers: 6 g Protein: 13 g

Dragon Bowl

I love colors, and Dragon Bowls offer endless possibilities when it comes to colorful plating. Use the vegetables you already have at home. I decided to give my recipe an Asian twist by combining tofu, sesame, coconut, and bok choy. Use your inspiration and creativity to invent your own variation.

 2 servings • 15 minutes • 50 minutes

INGREDIENTS

For the dressing

2 tablespoons (30 mL) peanut butter or tahini (sesame butter)

2 tablespoons (30 mL) plain yogurt

1 tablespoon (15 mL) coconut milk (see note)

⅓ cup (80 mL) coconut water

1 teaspoon (5 mL) honey

To assemble the bowl

½ cup (125 mL) uncooked brown rice

1¼ cups (310 mL) water

2 slices (3½ ounces/100 g each) firm or extra-firm tofu

1 cup (250 mL) curly lettuce

1 cup (250 mL) shaved red cabbage

1 carrot, grated

½ avocado, sliced

1 fennel bulb, coarsely chopped

1 red beet, thinly sliced

2 bok choy, coarsely chopped

Sesame seeds, for garnish

Note: You want only the solidified part of the coconut milk. Use the remaining liquid in smoothies or freeze it into cubes.

METHOD

1. Blend all the dressing ingredients together. Set aside.

2. Combine the rice with the 1¼ cups (310 mL) water in a small saucepan. Bring to a boil, stirring once or twice. Lower the heat, cover, and simmer 30 to 40 minutes or until the rice is tender and all the liquid is absorbed.

3. Meanwhile, brown the tofu slices in an oiled cast-iron skillet over medium heat.

4. Divide the cooked rice between two large serving bowls. Top with curly lettuce, red cabbage, carrot, avocado, fennel, beets, bok choy, and tofu.

5. Drizzle with some of the dressing, sprinkle with sesame seeds, and serve.

Hubert's Tip: *Think of adding a portion of starch to your lunches. Brown rice adds carbohydrates and fiber to this recipe. Another good option is wild rice.*

Nutritional value (per serving)
Calories: 609   Total fat: 28.7 g   Saturated fats: 9.7 g   Cholesterol: 1 mg
Sodium: 199 mg   Carbohydrates: 76 g   Fibers: 16 g   Protein: 25 g

Spicy Yogurt Sauce

I love Mexican food! When I don't know what to make for dinner, I'll often end up making fajitas with homemade guacamole. I also like spicy food, but not to the point of numbing my taste buds. This sauce is moderately spicy and perfect as a condiment to all Mexican dishes.

4 servings   10 minutes   5 minutes

INGREDIENTS

¼ cup (60 mL) cream (15% milk fat)

4 extra-spicy dry chili peppers

1 teaspoon (5 mL) Sriracha sauce

¼ cup (60 mL) light sour cream

¼ cup (60 mL) plain Greek yogurt

METHOD

1. Pour the cream into a saucepan and add the chili peppers. Bring to a slow boil, then simmer for about 5 minutes.

2. Let the cream cool for a few minutes, then whisk in the Sriracha sauce.

3. In a bowl, combine the sour cream and yogurt.

4. Gradually whisk the chili-infused cream into the yogurt mixture.

5. Serve cold with a Mexican salad, fajitas, or nachos.

Nutritional value (for ¼ of the sauce)
Calories: 56   Total fat: 4.3 g   Saturated fats: 2.6 g   Cholesterol: 14 mg
Sodium: 23 mg   Carbohydrates: 2 g   Fibers: 0 g   Protein: 2 g

Smoked Salmon

½ bagel, toasted

5 slices smoked salmon

Microgreens

1 tablespoon (15 mL) cream cheese mixed with 1 tablespoon (15 mL) yogurt, strained (p. 19)

Salt and pepper, to taste

Updated and Improved Sandwiches

Tuna

1 slice pumpernickel bread (German rye bread)

One 3.15-ounce (90 g) can yellowfin tuna, crumbled

2 tablespoons (30 mL) yogurt mayonnaise (p. 19)

Radishes, thinly sliced

Soybean sprouts

Salt and pepper, to taste

Grilled Chicken

1 slice whole wheat bread

5 slices grilled chicken

2 tablespoons (30 mL) yogurt mayonnaise (p. 19), seasoned with curry powder and turmeric

Kale leaves

Salt and pepper, to taste

Falafel

1 pita bread

3 green falafel (p. 67)

2 tablespoons (30 mL) tzatziki

Microgreens or alfalfa

Hulled Barley-Stuffed Bell Peppers

I've always loved my father's meat-stuffed tomatoes and bell peppers. The dish was his creative way to make us eat vegetables. I've updated the classic recipe by replacing the meat with a hulled barley and pesto filling.

4 servings   20 minutes   65 minutes

INGREDIENTS

1 cup (250 mL) uncooked hulled barley

4 bell peppers, various colors

½ cup (125 mL) pesto

⅓ cup (80 mL) plain, high-fat Greek yogurt

8 sun-dried tomatoes, julienned

Meat from 2 large Italian pork or veal sausages

1 cup (250 mL) shredded light mozzarella cheese

METHOD

1. Preheat the oven to 350°F (180°C).
2. Rinse the barley thoroughly. Transfer to a saucepan and cover with 2 inches (5 cm) of water. Bring to a boil, then reduce heat to medium-low, cover, and cook for 30 to 45 minutes.
3. While the barley is cooking, slice the bell peppers in half lengthwise and remove the cores.
4. Drain the cooked barley.
5. In a large mixing bowl, combine the cooked barley, pesto, yogurt, and sun-dried tomatoes. Fill the bell pepper halves with the barley mixture.
6. Top with crumbled sausage meat.
7. Bake for 20 minutes.
8. Remove from the oven. Sprinkle some of the cheese over each stuffed bell pepper. Broil for a few minutes or until the cheese is golden and bubbly.

Hubert's Tip: *You can add chopped nuts to the filling for a delightful crunch.*

Nutritional value (for 2 bell pepper halves)
Calories: 557 Total fat: 30.5 g Saturated fats: 9.7 g Cholesterol: 49 mg
Sodium: 471 mg Carbohydrates: 53 g Fibers: 11 g Protein: 21 g

Pasta, Seaweed, and Shrimp Salad

Pasta salad is a ubiquitous lunch dish, but my version has a little something extra. My secret ingredient is wakame, an edible seaweed frequently used in Japanese and Korean cuisine.

4 servings *15 minutes* *8 to 10 minutes*

INGREDIENTS

7 ounces (200 g) dry fusilli pasta

¼ cup (60 mL) plain Greek yogurt

2 tablespoons (30 mL) mayonnaise

24 cherry tomatoes, halved

2 stalks celery, diced

1 cucumber, diced

½ cup (125 mL) wakame

16 large shrimp, cooked

Sesame seeds (optional)

Salt and pepper, to taste

METHOD

1. In a large pot filled with salted water, cook the pasta according to the manufacturer's instructions. Drain, but do not rinse the pasta.

2. In a large mixing bowl, combine the Greek yogurt and mayonnaise. Add the vegetables and wakame, and mix to combine.

3. Fold in the pasta.

4. Season to taste, and divide among four serving bowls. Top with the shrimp, sprinkle with sesame seeds, if using, and season with salt and pepper to taste.

Hubert's Tip: *To increase your fiber intake, substitute half or all of the regular pasta with whole wheat pasta.*

Nutritional value (per serving)
Calories: 308 Total fat: 7.5 g Saturated fats: 1.3 g Cholesterol: 47 mg
Sodium: 199 mg Carbohydrates: 45 g Fibers: 4 g Protein: 15 g

Pulses and Friends

Pulses have been a mainstay in my diet for many years now. I like to use them in a variety of recipes: chili sin carne, hummus, and salads. Packed with fiber and proteins, which promote a feeling of satiety, pulses are an outstanding healthy ingredient that everyone should learn to cook with more often. This recipe was inspired by toasted coconut; the dressing has a subtle coconut flavor that transports me back to my vacations in the Caribbean.

4 servings   *15 minutes*

INGREDIENTS

For the salad

One 19-ounce (540 mL) can chickpeas, drained and rinsed

⅔ cup (160 mL) edamame beans

16 cherry tomatoes, quartered

Toasted coconut flakes, to taste

Juice from ½ lemon

Flat-leaf parsley, to taste

⅓ cup (80 mL) sunflower seeds

For the dressing

¼ cup (60 mL) plain Greek yogurt

2 tablespoons (30 mL) coconut milk

1 teaspoon (5 mL) Dijon mustard

1 teaspoon (5 mL) honey

Salt and pepper, to taste

METHOD

1. In a large mixing bowl, combine all the salad ingredients, except the sunflower seeds.
2. In a second bowl, whisk all the dressing ingredients together.
3. Divide the salad among four serving plates.
4. Drizzle some of the dressing over each plate and sprinkle with sunflower seeds.

Hubert's Tip: *This salad is great as a side dish. If you serve it as a side, ½ cup (125 mL) is an ideal portion.*

Nutritional value (per serving)
Calories: 306   Total fat: 12.5 g   Saturated fats: 2.9 g   Cholesterol: 1 mg
Sodium: 35 mg   Carbohydrates: 37 g   Fibers: 8 g   Protein: 16 g

Black Beans, Yogurt, and Mint

Sometimes the easiest recipes are also the most delicious. No need to rush to make this dish; all you need is 5 minutes to complete it from start to finish. The molasses adds a slightly caramelized and sweet taste.

4 servings   *5 minutes*

INGREDIENTS

One 19-ounce (540 mL) can black beans, drained and rinsed

2 tablespoons (30 mL) fancy molasses

1 cup (250 mL) plain Greek yogurt

Extra-virgin olive oil

1 lime, quartered

Fresh mint

Pinch of salt

METHOD

1. In a large mixing bowl, combine the black beans and molasses.

2. Divide the dressed black beans among serving plates.

3. Spoon ¼ cup (60 mL) yogurt over each black bean serving. Drizzle with olive oil and lime juice.

4. Garnish with fresh mint and season to taste.

Nutritional value (per serving)
Calories: 319   Total fat: 15.5 g   Saturated fats: 2.7 g   Cholesterol: 5 mg
Sodium: 69 mg   Carbohydrates: 32 g   Fibers: 7 g   Protein: 14 g

Deconstructed Green Plate

Green is the quintessential color of health. Green vegetables are packed with vitamins and minerals, and on top of that, they're delicious! In this recipe, I played with textures, flavors, and shades of green. My goal was to create a deconstructed salad that pleases the eye as much as the palate.

4 servings   *20 minutes*

INGREDIENTS

For the dressing

¼ cup (60 mL) cashews, soaked in water for a minimum of 4 hours

½ avocado

½ cup (125 mL) almond milk

¼ cup (60 mL) plain Greek yogurt

1 tablespoon (15 mL) nutritional yeast, or grated Parmesan cheese

½ teaspoon (2.5 mL) matcha green tea

For the green plate

8 mini bok choy

8 brussels sprouts

40 stalks asparagus

1 green bell pepper, cut into strips

1 broccoli, cut into florets

1 cup (250 mL) snow peas

½ cup (125 mL) soybean sprouts

1 cup (250 mL) edamame beans

METHOD

1. Place all the dressing ingredients in a blender and process to a smooth consistency.

2. Bring a large pot of water to a boil. Blanch all the vegetables for a few seconds, then transfer to a large bowl filled with ice water to cool. Drain thoroughly and dry the vegetables.

3. Carefully arrange the vegetables on a large serving plate and drizzle with the dressing.

Nutritional value (for ¼ of the dressing)
Calories: 100   Total fat: 7.9 g   Saturated fats: 1.4 g   Cholesterol: 1 mg
Sodium: 28 mg   Carbohydrates: 6 g   Fibers: 2 g   Protein: 4 g

3
Dinner

Butter Chicken

The aroma released during the preparation of this dish will fill your kitchen and transport you to South Asia. Butter chicken is all about the sauce: this recipe yields a great deal, so you can also dip your naan bread into it.

4 servings   20 minutes   15 minutes

INGREDIENTS

3 tablespoons (45 mL) butter

1 red onion, finely chopped

2 cloves garlic, minced

2 tablespoons (30 mL) tomato paste

1 teaspoon (5 mL) garam masala

Pinch of ground cinnamon

½ teaspoon (2.5 mL) finely grated fresh ginger

1 cup (250 mL) tomato sauce

1 tomato, diced

2 large chicken breasts (about 5 ounces/150 g each), cut in 1-inch (2.5 cm) cubes

¾ cup (180 mL) canned chickpeas, drained and rinsed

½ cup (125 mL) plain, high-fat Greek yogurt

¼ cup (60 mL) cream (15% milk fat)

Cilantro (optional, for garnish)

METHOD

1. In a nonstick skillet, melt the butter over medium heat. Sauté the onion until it is translucent.

2. Add the garlic, tomato paste, garam masala, cinnamon, and ginger, and cook for 1 minute. Add the tomato sauce and the diced tomato, and stir to combine.

3. Mix in the chicken and bring to a boil. Lower the heat to medium-low and simmer for 10 minutes, stirring often.

4. Add the chickpeas, yogurt, and cream, and mix to combine. Simmer for another minute, or until the chickpeas are warmed through.

5. Serve with naan bread and wild rice. Garnish with cilantro if desired.

Nutritional value (per serving)
Calories: 306 Total fat: 15.2 g Saturated fats: 8.6 g Cholesterol: 80 mg
Sodium: 483 mg Carbohydrates: 20 g Fibers: 3 g Protein: 23 g

Stuffed Shells with a Little Something Extra

When I was young, my parents wouldn't make lasagna at home, but rather would fill shell pasta with spinach and ricotta cheese. The two recipes have a lot in common, but I'm partial to shells because you can neatly pack them into a lunch, and you can easily serve portions tailored to each person's appetite. Dad and Mom can have between four and six, and the kids can have three apiece.

30 pasta shells (6 servings) *20 minutes* *20 minutes*

INGREDIENTS

30 dry extra-large pasta shells

1⅓ cups (320 mL) ricotta cheese

1½ cups (375 mL) Greek yogurt, strained (see instructions on p. 19)

2 cups (500 mL) chopped fresh spinach, or ¾ cup (180 mL) frozen spinach, thawed and drained thoroughly

1 cup (250 mL) grated carrot

2 cups (500 mL) meat or tomato sauce, either homemade or store-bought

1 cup (250 mL) shredded sharp cheddar

METHOD

1. Preheat the oven to 400°F (200°C).
2. Cook the pasta shells according to the manufacturer's instructions. Drain, but do not rinse the pasta.
3. In a large mixing bowl, combine the ricotta and Greek yogurt. Fold in the spinach, carrot, and half the meat sauce.
4. Fill each shell with the mixture, then set the shells side by side in a baking pan.
5. Pour the remaining sauce over the shells, and sprinkle with the cheese.
6. Bake for 15 minutes or until the cheese is golden and bubbly.

Hubert's Tip: *I like to add grated carrots to the filling, but other vegetables also work great. Try using red cabbage or broccoli stalks.*

Nutritional value (for 5 shells)
Calories: 390   Total fat: 17 g   Saturated fats: 10.2 g   Cholesterol: 63 mg
Sodium: 464 mg   Carbohydrates: 34 g   Fibers: 3 g   Protein: 25 g

Nutritional value (for 25 gnocchi)
Calories: 204   Total fat: 2 g   Saturated fats: 1.0 g   Cholesterol: 5 mg   Sodium: 106 mg   Carbohydrates: 39 g   Fibers: 4 g   Protein: 7 g

Sweet Potato Gnocchi

I love to make gnocchi, and I not only serve them the traditional way, with tomato sauce, but also add them to soups and salads. I like to add an array of flavors to my gnocchi dough, which also has the benefit of making them colorful. I especially like to make them with sweet potato, which provides a mild and slightly sweet flavor.

200 gnocchi, about 8 servings   *45 minutes*   *45 minutes*

INGREDIENTS

28 ounces (800 g) sweet potatoes (about 2 large)

¼ cup (60 mL) plain Greek yogurt

⅓ cup (80 mL) grated Parmesan cheese

½ teaspoon (2.5 mL) freshly grated nutmeg

½ teaspoon (2.5 mL) salt

1½ to 2 cups (375 to 500 mL) all-purpose flour (plus more for the work surface)

METHOD

1. Preheat the oven to 450°F (230°C).

2. Halve the sweet potatoes and bake them for 45 minutes or until the flesh is tender.

3. Let cool completely, then puree using a potato masher.

4. In a large mixing bowl, combine the mashed potatoes, yogurt, Parmesan, nutmeg, and salt.

5. Gradually mix in the flour, kneading the mixture into a dough until it is smooth but still slightly sticky.

6. Roll the dough into a ball, then cut it into four portions.

7. Using the palm of your hand, roll out one portion of dough to create a long rope, about ½ inch (1 cm) thick. Add more flour to your work surface as needed.

8. Cut the rope into ½-inch (1 cm) bites.

9. Roll each dough bite on a gnocchi plank or the back of a fork.

10. Repeat with the remaining sections of dough, and sprinkle some flour over the rolled gnocchi to prevent them from sticking to one another.

11. To cook the gnocchi, bring a large pot of salted water to a boil. Lower the heat slightly. Drop the gnocchi into the water and cook for 3 to 4 minutes or until they float back to the surface. This will happen quickly, so keep watch.

12. Alternatively, to freeze the uncooked gnocchi for future use, set them on a baking sheet and freeze for 30 minutes. When the gnocchi are frozen and firm, transfer them to airtight bags and keep frozen until ready to use.

Creamy Carbonara Tagliatelle

When I host friends for dinner, I sometimes feel like serving a deliciously rich and creamy pasta dish, but the sauces of such dishes can be a bit too rich, calorie-wise. To enjoy the experience of carbonara pasta without the guilt, I came up with clever substitutions, such as using crispy prosciutto instead of the usual bacon. It's a delight!

 4 servings   15 minutes   15 minutes

INGREDIENTS

2 tablespoons (30 mL) butter

1 teaspoon (5 mL) minced garlic

¼ cup (60 mL) milk

¼ cup (60 mL) cream (15% milk fat)

¾ cup (180 mL) plain Greek yogurt

½ cup (125 mL) grated Parmesan cheese

Salt and pepper, to taste

10½ ounces (300 g) dry tagliatelle pasta

5 ounces (150 g) prosciutto or Parma ham

Chopped chives, for garnish

Fresh or dried thyme, for garnish

METHOD

1. Preheat the oven to 350°F (180°C).
2. In a saucepan, melt the butter over medium heat. Add the garlic.
3. Whisk in the milk and cream. Bring to a boil, then remove from the heat and let cool for 2 to 3 minutes.
4. Gradually whisk in the yogurt, then the Parmesan cheese. Mix until the cheese is melted. Season to taste, and set aside.
5. Cook the pasta according to the manufacturer's instructions.
6. While the pasta cooks, place the prosciutto on a baking sheet lined with parchment paper. Bake in the preheated oven for 10 minutes or until the prosciutto is crispy.
7. Drain the cooked pasta, but do not rinse.
8. Transfer the pasta to the saucepan with the sauce, and mix to coat the pasta.
9. Divide the pasta among four serving plates. Top with crispy prosciutto, chives, and thyme.

Hubert's Tip: *Serving for serving, prosciutto contains half the calories and three times less fat than bacon does.*

Nutritional value (per serving)
Calories: 530   Total fat: 18.1 g   Saturated fats: 9.5 g   Cholesterol: 78 mg
Sodium: 1,110 mg   Carbohydrates: 60 g   Fibers: 3 g   Protein: 29 g

Braised Beef Shepherd's Pie

I've been eating shepherd's pie my whole life. Pâté chinois, as it is known in French, is a traditional Québécois dish, much like poutine. Of course, Québécois cuisine can be much more refined than that, but I still love these classic comfort-food dishes. In this recipe, I use beef braised in dark beer instead of the usual ground beef, and I add yogurt and parsnips to the mashed potatoes. These small changes truly elevate the dish!

 6 servings   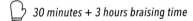 30 minutes   30 minutes + 3 hours braising time

INGREDIENTS

For the braised beef

28 ounces (800 g) beef chuck

¼ cup (60 mL) balsamic vinegar

1 clove garlic

2 onions, chopped

Fresh or dried thyme, to taste

One 15.2-ounce (450 mL) bottle dark beer

Salt and pepper, to taste

For the mashed potatoes and to assemble

3 cups (750 mL) peeled and chopped potatoes

2 cups (500 mL) peeled and chopped parsnips

2 tablespoons (30 mL) butter

½ cup (125 mL) plain Greek yogurt

One 10-ounce (284 mL) can creamed corn

One 11½-ounce (341 mL) can corn kernels

Smoked paprika, for garnish

Thyme (optional, for garnish)

METHOD

For the braised beef

1. Preheat the oven to 350°F (180°C).

2. In a large, oiled ovenproof pot with a tight-fitting lid, brown the beef over medium-high heat, about 5 minutes on each side.

3. Remove the meat and deglaze the pot with balsamic vinegar.

4. Add the garlic, onions, thyme, beer, salt, and pepper, and return the meat to the pot. Cover tightly with the lid. Braise in the oven for 3 hours or until you can shred the meat with a fork.

For the mashed potatoes, and to assemble the dish

5. Preheat the oven to 350°F (180°C).

6. Place the chopped potatoes and parsnips in a large pot, cover with water, and bring to a boil. Cook until the vegetables are tender, about 20 minutes. Drain and let cool completely.

7. Mash the vegetables using a potato masher. Add the butter and yogurt, and mix to combine. Set aside.

8. Spread the shredded braised beef over the bottom of a 10- × 15-inch (25 × 38 cm) baking pan.

9. Combine the creamed corn with the corn kernels and spread over the beef layer. Top with a layer of potato and parsnip puree.

10. Sprinkle with smoked paprika and bake for 30 minutes. Garnish with fresh thyme.

Nutritional value (per serving)
Calories: 416   Total fat: 9.7 g   Saturated fats: 4.4 g   Cholesterol: 100 mg
Sodium: 186 mg   Carbohydrates: 38 g   Fibers: 4 g   Protein: 43 g

Coquilles Saint-Jacques

I've long had a love-hate relationship with scallops. The day I was served overcooked, tough scallops, I swore that I'd had it with this seafood. But because my love for cooking (and food!) is unconditional, I later learned to cook scallops like a chef would. Au gratin scallops, or coquilles Saint-Jacques, as the dish is called in French, is now one of my favorite meals.

4 servings   *20 minutes*   *30 minutes*

INGREDIENTS

For the potato and cauliflower puree

2 cups (500 mL) peeled and chopped potatoes

2 cups (500 mL) chopped cauliflower

¼ cup (60 mL) butter

½ cup (125 mL) plain Greek yogurt

For the yogurt béchamel

1½ cups (375 mL) milk

½ cup (125 mL) cream (15% milk fat)

½ teaspoon (2.5 mL) freshly grated nutmeg

2 tablespoons (30 mL) butter

2 tablespoons (30 mL) all-purpose flour

¾ cup (180 mL) plain, high-fat Greek yogurt

Salt and pepper, to taste

For the scallops

16 large scallops

2 tablespoons (30 mL) butter

Salt and pepper, to taste

Sage, for garnish

METHOD

For the potato and cauliflower puree

1. Place the potatoes and cauliflower in a large pot filled with salted water, and bring to a boil. Cook until the vegetables are tender, about 20 minutes. Drain and let cool completely.
2. Puree the vegetables using a potato masher.
3. Add the butter and yogurt, and mix to combine. Set aside.

For the yogurt béchamel

4. In a saucepan, combine the milk, cream, and nutmeg. Set the saucepan over medium heat for 5 minutes or until the mixture simmers. Remove from the heat and set aside.
5. In a nonstick skillet over medium heat, prepare a roux with the butter and flour. To do this, add the flour to the butter, all at once, stirring continuously with a wooden spoon for 2 minutes. Lower the heat to medium-low and slowly pour the hot milk mixture into the skillet, whisking constantly to incorporate.
6. Simmer for 10 minutes, then remove from the heat and let cool for a few minutes. Whisk in the yogurt and season to taste.

To assemble the dish

7. Fill a pastry bag fitted with an open-star tip with the potato and cauliflower puree. Divide the puree among four ovenproof shell-shaped dishes or plates.
8. Broil the puree until golden, about 3 to 5 minutes.
9. In a cast-iron skillet, sear the scallops 1½ minutes on each side. Place four scallops in the center of each serving dish, over the puree. Cover with béchamel sauce, and season to taste. Garnish with sage.

Nutritional value (per serving)
Calories: 498 Total fat: 32.5 g Saturated fats: 19.9 g Cholesterol: 112 mg
Sodium: 205 mg Carbohydrates: 30 g Fibers: 2 g Protein: 22 g

Salmon Tartare with Citrus Fruit Supremes

I'm crazy for tartare. I have long refrained from making it at home because I thought it was a complicated dish, and I was wary that the result wouldn't be worthy of the best versions I'd had in restaurants. I've since discovered that all you need is the right recipe, and boom—you can't stop making it at home! I like all variations of salmon tartare, but I have to say, grapefruit and fennel fronds make this one exceptional.

2 servings   *30 minutes*

INGREDIENTS

1 orange, supremed (see note)

½ grapefruit, supremed (see note)

Seeds of ½ pomegranate, plus more for garnish

10½ ounces (300 g) sushi-grade salmon, raw

2 tablespoons (30 mL) yogurt mayonnaise (p. 19)

½ teaspoon (2.5 mL) seasoned rice vinegar

Fennel fronds (or dill), plus more for garnish

Salt and pepper, to taste

Sriracha sauce, to taste

Note: To prepare the orange (and grapefruit) supreme, cut off the top and bottom of the orange until you can see the flesh of the fruit. Place the fruit on one end and with a paring knife, remove the peel and all the pith (the white parts). Then, to extract the segments without getting any of the membrane, run the knife between each orange wedge to separate the flesh of the fruit from the membrane.

METHOD

1. Dice the orange and grapefruit supremes and transfer to a bowl. Mix in the pomegranate seeds. Set aside.

2. Use a sharp knife to dice the salmon.

3. In a large mixing bowl, gently combine the salmon, yogurt mayonnaise, seasoned rice vinegar, fennel fronds, salt, pepper, and Sriracha sauce. Taste to verify the seasoning and adjust it if needed.

4. Use a round cookie cutter to serve the tartare in a neat round shape. (If you don't have a cookie cutter, you can also use a ramekin.)

5. Divide the fruit mixture between two plates and top with the salmon tartare. Garnish with fennel fronds and pomegranate seeds and serve immediately.

Hubert's Tip: *Salmon is full of omega-3 fatty acids, good fats that, among other things, help to decrease the level of triglycerides in blood and improve mood. It is recommended to have two portions of fish per week.*

Nutritional value (per serving)
Calories: 288 Total fat: 11.7 g Saturated fats: 1.9 g Cholesterol: 84 mg
Sodium: 82 mg Carbohydrates: 14 g Fibers: 3 g Protein: 31 g

Fig Focaccia

Are you intimidated by the idea of making focaccia from scratch? I was skeptical, too—but that was before I made this recipe. Because focaccia dough doesn't need to rise, you can make it incredibly quickly and have fun by varying the flavors you add to the dough and the ingredients you choose for the topping. Huzzah for focaccia!

4 servings   15 minutes   5 minutes for the dough + 7 to 8 minutes for the focaccia

INGREDIENTS

For the focaccia

1 cup (250 mL) all-purpose flour

½ cup (125 mL) buckwheat flour

½ cup (125 mL) whole wheat flour

1 teaspoon (5 mL) baking powder

1 cup (250 mL) plain Greek yogurt (0% milk fat)

¼ cup (60 mL) chopped black olives

1 teaspoon (5 mL) dried basil

Pinch of salt

For the topping

¾ cup (180 mL) tomato sauce

6 fresh figs, quartered

1 small red onion, finely chopped

¼ cup (60 mL) sliced black olives

2½ ounces (70 g) goat cheese, crumbled

2 tablespoons (30 mL) pumpkin seeds

Fresh basil leaves

Hubert's Tip: *Use focaccia dough as a base for pizza!*

METHOD

For the focaccia

1. Preheat the oven to 425°F (220°C).
2. In a large mixing bowl, combine the flours, baking powder, and yogurt. Knead into a dough that is neither too firm nor too sticky. Add a bit of water if the dough is too dry, or sprinkle a bit more flour if the dough is too sticky.
3. Fold in the black olives, dried basil, and salt.
4. On a floured work surface, use a rolling pin to roll out the dough to form an 8- × 14-inch (20 × 35 cm) rectangle. Using your fingers, shape the edge of the dough to form the crust.
5. Transfer the focaccia to a baking sheet lined with parchment paper.
6. Using a fork, prick the dough all over to prevent bubbles from forming during the baking process.
7. Bake for 5 minutes.
8. Take out of the oven and let cool for a few minutes.

For the topping

9. Distribute the tomato sauce, fresh figs, red onion, black olives, goat cheese, and pumpkin seeds all over the focaccia.
10. Bake for 7 to 8 more minutes.
11. Top with fresh basil leaves right before serving.

Nutritional value (per serving)
Calories: 463   Total fat: 12.6 g   Saturated fats: 5.3 g   Cholesterol: 19 mg
Sodium: 686 mg   Carbohydrates: 70 g   Fibers: 8 g   Protein: 20 g

Yogurt, Tomato, and Braised Lamb Risotto

Buying a cast-iron casserole pot made me fall in love with braised meats. Whatever meat you use, you're guaranteed that the dish is going to be a hit. I have a soft spot for lamb shank, which is such a tender and tasty meat. Served with risotto, it's a popular, festive dish! Make sure to cook more rice than you actually need so you can turn leftovers into arancini, the irresistible Sicilian rice balls.

 4 servings   20 minutes   4 hours

INGREDIENTS

For the braised lamb

2 tablespoons (30 mL) extra virgin olive oil

4 lamb shanks

1 medium onion, finely chopped

2 cups (500 mL) red wine

1 cup (250 mL) beef broth

6 Italian tomatoes, halved

For the risotto

3 tablespoons (45 mL) butter

2 shallots, finely chopped

2 cloves garlic, finely chopped

1¾ cups (425 mL) arborio or carnaroli rice

½ cup (125 mL) white wine

6 cups (1.5 L) chicken broth, divided

Grated Parmesan cheese, to taste

3 tablespoons (45 mL) cooking cream (15% milk fat)

½ cup (125 mL) plain, high-fat Greek yogurt

Salt and pepper, to taste

Sprigs of parsley, for garnish

METHOD

For the braised lamb

1. Preheat the oven to 250°F (120°C).

2. In a cast-iron casserole pot with a tight-fitting lid, heat the oil and brown the lamb shanks on all sides. Remove the lamb shanks from the pot and set aside.

3. Add the onion to the pot and sauté for 2 minutes.

4. Add the lamb shanks back to the casserole, then add the red wine, beef broth, and tomatoes. Cover and bake for 4 hours.

5. Shred the meat and set aside.

For the risotto

6. Start the risotto about 30 minutes before the lamb has finished braising. In a large pot, melt the butter over medium heat, and sauté the shallots and garlic.

7. Add the rice and stir until the grains become translucent, about 5 minutes.

8. Add the white wine, and stir until the wine has completely evaporated.

9. Add a cup of chicken broth, and simmer over low heat, stirring regularly. As soon as all the liquid is absorbed, add another cup of broth. Repeat until the risotto is creamy but still al dente.

10. Stir in the Parmesan cheese, cream, and yogurt, and season with salt and pepper to taste.

11. Divide the risotto among serving plates. Top with shredded braised lamb and some of the braising sauce, and garnish with parsley.

Nutritional value (per serving)
Calories: 650   Total fat: 24.9 g   Saturated fats: 10.9 g   Cholesterol: 101 mg
Sodium: 977 mg   Carbohydrates: 56 g   Fibers: 4 g   Protein: 45 g

lobster Vol-Au-Vent

I feel lucky that my father is from Havre-Saint-Pierre, a tiny coastal village on Québec's North Shore that makes its living mostly from the fishery and other natural resources. When I was growing up, we would visit the village in the summer and go to the port's fish market to get fresh lobsters. We would then bring our "catch" to my grandmother, who cooked them to perfection. Every year, when lobster season comes around, these fond childhood memories return to me. Here's a comforting way to enjoy lobster: in a silky sauce served over a puff pastry shell.

 4 servings 15 minutes 🧤 20 minutes

INGREDIENTS

For the yogurt béchamel

1½ cups (375 mL) milk

½ cup (125 mL) cream (15% milk fat)

4 whole cloves

2 tablespoons (30 mL) butter

2 tablespoons (30 mL) all-purpose flour

¾ cup (180 mL) plain, high-fat Greek yogurt

Salt and pepper, to taste

To assemble

4 puff pastry shells

12 ounces (375 g) lobster meat, in chunks

1 cup (250 mL) green peas

Hubert's Tip: *Seafood is an excellent source of lean protein. In this recipe, you could use crab, scallops, or cold-water shrimp in place of the lobster.*

METHOD

For the yogurt béchamel

1. In a saucepan, combine the milk, cream, and cloves. Set the saucepan over medium heat for 5 minutes or until the mixture simmers. Remove from the heat and set aside.

2. In a nonstick skillet over medium heat, prepare a roux with the butter and flour. To do this, add the flour to the butter, all at once, stirring continuously with a wooden spoon for 2 minutes.

3. Lower the heat to medium-low and slowly pour the hot milk mixture into the skillet, whisking constantly to incorporate. Season to taste.

4. Simmer for 10 minutes, then remove from the heat and let cool for a few minutes. Stir in the yogurt, and season to taste.

To assemble the vol-au-vent

5. Place a pastry shell in the center of each plate.

6. Top each pastry shell with a quarter of the lobster meat.

7. Reheat the béchamel sauce, if needed, and spoon it over each lobster-filled shell. Sprinkle each with green peas.

8. For an appealing finishing touch, top with more lobster meat (the claws, for example).

Nutritional value (per serving)
Calories: 521   Total fat: 30.5 g   Saturated fats: 11.1 g   Cholesterol: 110 mg
Sodium: 528 mg   Carbohydrates: 32 g   Fibers: 1 g   Protein: 28 g

Grilled Meat with Blue Cheese
Sauce and Roasted Cauliflower
(see recipe on following page)

Grilled Meat with Blue Cheese Sauce and Roasted Cauliflower

Like many of you, I'm sure, I've long been reluctant to eat blue cheese, but once I tried it, I discovered I had been missing out on an excellent cheese! It's a perfect match with any grilled meat. Here's a dish one might say is typical "man food": a huge piece of rare meat accompanied by a tasty blue cheese sauce and some spectacular roasted cauliflower. Everyone will love it!

 4 servings 20 minutes 25 minutes

INGREDIENTS

For the blue cheese sauce

⅓ cup (80 mL) crumbled blue cheese

2 cups (500 mL) plain, high-fat Greek yogurt

2 green onions, finely chopped

1 stalk celery, finely chopped

Juice from ½ lemon

1 tablespoon (15 mL) Worcestershire sauce

Salt and pepper, to taste

For the roasted cauliflower

1 large head cauliflower

4 servings grilled meat of your choice

METHOD

For the blue cheese sauce

1. In a large mixing bowl, combine the blue cheese, yogurt, green onions, celery, lemon juice, and Worcestershire sauce. Season to taste, and refrigerate until ready to use.

For the roasted cauliflower

2. Preheat the oven to 450°F (230°C).

3. Blanch the cauliflower head (including the leaves) by plunging it in a large pot of boiling water for 1 minute. Drain and dry thoroughly.

4. Place the cauliflower head on a baking sheet and roast for 25 minutes (the cooking time will vary according to the size of the cauliflower head).

5. Serve with grilled meat and the blue cheese sauce.

Hubert's Tip: *The blue cheese sauce is equally great with red meats or grilled poultry.*

Nutritional value (for ¼ of the sauce)
Calories: 184   Total fat: 11 g   Saturated fats: 7.1 g   Cholesterol: 32 mg
Sodium: 247 mg   Carbohydrates: 12 g   Fibers: 1 g   Protein: 8 g

Stuffed Potatoes

This may sound surprising, but I'm not generally a big fan of potatoes or French fries . . .
but this recipe is nothing short of amazing! We're a long way from the traditional
baked potato stuffed with cheese, bacon, and sour cream. This recipe is a completely reinvented,
healthier version of the classic dish.

 4 servings   15 minutes   50 minutes

INGREDIENTS

4 russet potatoes

1½ cups (375 mL) chopped spinach

½ cup (125 mL) crumbled feta cheese

¼ cup (60 mL) pitted black olives

6 sun-dried tomatoes, drained and chopped

½ cup (125 mL) plain Greek yogurt

1 tablespoon (15 mL) extra virgin olive oil

Salt and pepper, to taste

METHOD

1. Preheat the oven to 400°F (200°C).

2. Using a fork or the pointy tip of a knife, prick the potatoes all over. Wrap them individually in aluminum foil.

3. Bake for 50 minutes or until the potatoes are tender. Remove from the oven and let cool for a few minutes.

4. Cut each potato in half lengthwise. Using a small spoon, carefully scoop out the potato flesh, making sure to leave a ½-inch (1 cm) "wall" all around.

5. Mash the scooped-out flesh using a potato masher. Mix in the chopped spinach, feta cheese, black olives, sun-dried tomatoes, yogurt, and olive oil. Season with salt and pepper to taste.

6. Scoop the filling back into the potato shells, and serve.

Nutritional value (per serving)
Calories: 242   Total fat: 10 g   Saturated fats: 4 g   Cholesterol: 20 mg
Sodium: 337 mg   Carbohydrates: 30 g   Fibers: 3 g   Protein: 9 g

Crispy Chicken

This recipe comes from a good friend of mine. I love General Tso's chicken, but I don't digest fried foods well; they often make me feel bloated. My friend convinced me to try her version of the dish, which surprisingly uses crushed puffed rice cereal for the breading. I've never looked back! The only elements I play around with are the spices, according to my whims.

4 servings   5 minutes   2 to 3 hours   15 minutes

INGREDIENTS

1 cup (250 mL) plain Greek yogurt

2 teaspoons (10 mL) ground cumin

2 large chicken breasts (about 5 ounces/150 g each), cut in 1-inch (2.5 cm) cubes

2 cups (500 mL) puffed rice cereal (such as Rice Krispies)

METHOD

1. In a bowl, combine the yogurt, cumin, and chicken. Cover with plastic wrap and leave to marinate in the refrigerator for 2 to 3 hours.

2. Preheat the oven to 400°F (200°C).

3. Scoop the puffed rice cereal into a resealable plastic bag. Use a rolling pin to crush the cereal lightly.

4. Transfer the crumbs to a plate and dredge the chicken pieces into it, one by one.

5. Place the chicken pieces on a baking sheet and bake for 15 minutes or until the crumbs are golden. Turn over the pieces halfway through the cooking time.

Hubert's Tip: *Add ground pecans or walnuts to the puffed rice crumbs for an even crispier texture.*

Nutritional value (per serving)
Calories: 206   Total fat: 5.1 g   Saturated fats: 2.8 g   Cholesterol: 55 mg
Sodium: 236 mg   Carbohydrates: 17 g   Fibers: 0 g   Protein: 21 g

Vitamin-Packed Sweet Potato Sauté

I like family-style meals where all dishes are set in the middle of the table. It's a friendly type of experience, as everyone can help themselves to the food they feel like eating. This dish fits exactly into such a spread. Filled with flavor, color, and vitamins, it's a crowd pleaser.

4 servings   15 minutes   40 minutes

INGREDIENTS

1 large sweet potato, cubed

¼ cup (60 mL) plain Greek yogurt

1 clove garlic, minced

1 tablespoon (15 mL) butter

Salt and pepper, to taste

8 cherry tomatoes

8 brussels sprouts

1 red bell pepper, cut into strips

1 zucchini, cut into rounds

Pearl onions, to taste

Snow peas, to taste

1 cup (250 mL) chopped kale

METHOD

1. In a large pot, boil the sweet potato cubes until tender. Drain.
2. Using a potato masher, mash the sweet potato. Mix in the yogurt, garlic, and butter. Season to taste.
3. In a lightly oiled cast-iron skillet, sear the other vegetables.
4. Spread the sweet potato puree onto a large serving plate, then top with the seared vegetables.

Hubert's Tip: *Use yogurt instead of butter, sour cream, or heavy cream in vegetable purees. The texture will be just as pleasant, but the fat content will be considerably lower.*

Nutritional value (per serving)
Calories: 176   Total fat: 1.1 g   Saturated fats: 0.3 g   Cholesterol: 2 mg
Sodium: 75 mg   Carbohydrates: 37 g   Fibers: 8 g   Protein: 7 g

Duck Breast Poutine

Everyone knows poutine is a classic of Québécois cuisine. What you may not know is that many of us Québécois also like to make poutine at home, using our favorite ingredients as toppings. Like many chefs have done before me, I decided to create a gastronomic version of the dish, by using duck breast as the central ingredient. This is certainly the most decadent dish in the entire book!

 4 servings   25 minutes   45 minutes

INGREDIENTS

For the fries

4 to 5 potatoes, scrubbed clean and cut into ½-inch (1 cm) sticks

3 tablespoons (45 mL) extra virgin olive oil

Fresh thyme leaves or ½ teaspoon (2.5 mL) dried thyme

For the sauce

2 tablespoons (30 mL) duck fat

2 shallots, finely chopped

1 clove garlic, finely chopped

1 cup (250 mL) white wine

2 tablespoons (30 mL) whole-grain mustard

1 cup (250 mL) cream (15% milk fat)

½ cup (125 mL) plain, high-fat Greek yogurt

½ cup (125 mL) duck stock (or veal stock)

For the duck

2 tablespoons (30 mL) extra virgin olive oil

10½ ounces (300 g) duck breast

1 cup (250 mL) cheese curds

Fresh thyme leaves, for garnish

METHOD

For the fries

1. Preheat the oven to 400°F (200°C).
2. In a resealable plastic bag, mix the potato sticks, olive oil, and thyme.
3. Transfer the potato sticks to a baking sheet lined with parchment paper, and bake for 45 minutes or until the fries are golden.

For the sauce

4. Meanwhile, in a nonstick skillet, melt the duck fat and brown the shallots and garlic. Deglaze with the white wine and reduce. Whisk in the whole-grain mustard, cream, yogurt, and duck stock. Reduce until the sauce has a creamy consistency. Keep warm.

For the duck

5. In a stainless-steel skillet, heat the olive oil and sear the duck breast for 5 minutes on each side. Wrap the duck breast in aluminum foil and let rest for 6 to 7 minutes. Slice the duck breast thinly.
6. Place the fries on a large plate. Top with cheese curds and duck breast slices. Pour some of the sauce over the poutine, and garnish with thyme leaves.

Nutritional value (per serving)
Calories: 977 Total fat: 53.8 g Saturated fats: 24.3 g Cholesterol: 163 mg
Sodium: 526 mg Carbohydrates: 72 g Fibers: 7 g Protein: 41 g

4

Snacks

Frozen Bars

When it's hot outside and the sun's rays are beating down on you, you need to find a way to refresh yourself. For some, taking a plunge in a pool or in the ocean does the trick, but for those who live in the city like me, without easy access to water, frozen bars are the perfect way to cool down. You can be creative when it comes to flavors: I dared to add carrots to mine!
Will you notice them?

 12 frozen bars   10 minutes   4 hours

INGREDIENTS

1 mango, peeled and pitted

2 oranges, supremed (see note on p. 103)

1 cup (250 mL) grated carrot

1 banana

¾ cup (180 mL) apple juice

¾ cup (180 mL) plain Greek yogurt

1 tablespoon (15 mL) honey

12 popsicle sticks

METHOD

1. Process all the ingredients in a food processor.

2. Pour into frozen bar molds and add one stick to each bar.

3. Freeze for about 4 hours.

Hubert's Tip: *The protein, calcium, bioactive peptides, amino acids, and fatty acids contained in yogurt are believed to play an important role in weight loss.[8] So don't hesitate to add yogurt to your frozen bars and smoothies!*

Nutritional value (per frozen bar)
Calories: 58   Total fat: 0.5 g   Saturated fats: 0.2 g   Cholesterol: 1 mg
Sodium: 12 mg   Carbohydrates: 13 g   Fibers: 2 g   Protein: 2 g

Apple, Hummus, and Chocolate Rolls

I discovered this recipe during a trip to Newfoundland. I was there to attend a nutrition conference, and I had a few days to tour the area. I even hopped on a boat expedition on the Atlantic Ocean in a quest to see icebergs! After we returned to the coast, I stopped at a small restaurant run by a young hipster couple who specialized in making hummus. They offered a wide variety of hummus creations, including one flavored with chocolate. It was served spread on rice noodle wrappers and topped with apple slices. Here's my version of this fun find.

12 rolls   *20 minutes*

INGREDIENTS

1 Granny Smith apple

Water

Juice from 1 lemon

Six 1-ounce squares (10 g each) dark chocolate

One 19-ounce (540 mL) can black beans, drained and rinsed

⅓ cup (80 mL) plain Greek yogurt (2% milk fat)

2 tablespoons (30 mL) cocoa powder

1 tablespoon (15 mL) honey

½ teaspoon (2.5 mL) ground cinnamon

12 small rice paper wrappers

Warm water

METHOD

1. Use a mandolin to slice the apple thinly.
2. Dip the apple slices in a bowl of water combined with the lemon juice so they don't brown.
3. In a double boiler, melt the dark chocolate. Set aside.
4. In a food processor, add the black beans, yogurt, melted dark chocolate, cocoa powder, honey, and cinnamon. Process until the mixture is smooth.
5. Dip a rice paper wrapper in a bowl of warm water for a few seconds.
6. Place two slices of apple over the rice paper wrapper. Spread some of the chocolate hummus over the apples, and roll like you would a spring roll.
7. Serve immediately, or keep in fridge for up to 3 days.

Nutritional value (for 2 rolls)
Calories: 211   Total fat: 5.2 g   Saturated fats: 2.9 g   Cholesterol: 2 mg
Sodium: 24 mg   Carbohydrates: 34 g   Fibers: 7 g   Protein: 9 g

Beet Hummus

Baba
Ghanoush

"Cheflor"
Dip

Edamame
Dip

(see recipes on
following spread)

Baba Ghanoush

♀♀ 4 servings 🥛 5 minutes 🌡 15 mins 🧤 30 minutes

INGREDIENTS

2 small eggplants

1 tablespoon (15 mL) extra virgin olive oil

Juice from ½ lemon

¼ cup (60 mL) tahini (sesame butter)

1 teaspoon (5 mL) minced garlic

¼ cup (60 mL) plain Greek yogurt

Salt and pepper, to taste

For garnish

Fresh cilantro leaves

Cold-pressed olive oil

2 cloves roasted garlic

Soybean sprouts

METHOD

1. Preheat the oven to 400°F (200°C).

2. Halve the eggplants lengthwise and cut slits into the skin. Brush with olive oil and place on a baking sheet, flesh side down. Bake for 30 minutes, then let cool for 15 minutes.

3. Use a spoon to scoop out the eggplant flesh, then squeeze lemon juice over top so that the flesh doesn't brown.

4. In a food processor, add the eggplant flesh, tahini, garlic, and yogurt, and process until the mixture is smooth.

5. Season with salt and pepper. Transfer to a serving bowl and garnish as desired.

Nutritional value (per serving)
Calories: 162 Total fat: 12 g Saturated fats: 1.8 g Cholesterol: 1 mg
Sodium: 9 mg Carbohydrates: 12 g Fibers: 6 g Protein: 5 g

Beet Hummus

♀♀ 4 servings 🥛 5 minutes

INGREDIENTS

½ cup (125 mL) canned chickpeas, drained and rinsed

1 cooked red beet

2 tablespoons (30 mL) plain Greek yogurt

2 tablespoons (30 mL) sesame oil

Salt and pepper, to taste

For garnish

Crumbled feta cheese

Roasted chickpeas

Smoked paprika

Fresh basil leaves

Cold-pressed olive oil

METHOD

1. In the bowl of a food processor, add the chickpeas, beet, yogurt, and sesame oil, and process until smooth.

2. Season with salt and pepper. Transfer to a serving bowl and garnish as desired.

Nutritional value (per serving)
Calories: 107 Total fat: 7.6 g Saturated fats: 1.1 g Cholesterol: 0 mg
Sodium: 14 mg Carbohydrates: 7 g Fibers: 1 g Protein: 3 g

"Cheflor" Dip

 4 servings   5 minutes   10 minutes

INGREDIENTS

8 ounces (225 g) cauliflower, chopped into pieces (about 1 medium head cauliflower)

2 tablespoons (30 mL) almond butter

1 teaspoon (5 mL) minced garlic

2 teaspoons (10 mL) ground cumin

¼ cup (60 mL) yogurt, strained (see instructions on p. 19)

Juice from ½ lemon

Salt and pepper, to taste

For garnish

Grated carrot

Toasted sliced almonds

Jalapeño pepper

Extra virgin olive oil

METHOD

1. Cook the cauliflower in boiling water until tender, about 10 minutes.
2. In a food processor, add all the ingredients except salt, pepper, and garnishes, and process until smooth.
3. Season with salt and pepper. Transfer to a serving bowl and garnish as desired.

Nutritional value (per serving)
Calories: 67 Total fat: 5.1 g Saturated fats: 0.5 g Cholesterol: 0 mg
Sodium: 10 mg Carbohydrates: 5 g Fibers: 2 g Protein: 2 g

Edamame Dip

4 servings   5 minutes

INGREDIENTS

1½ cups (375 mL) edamame beans

2 tablespoons (30 mL) plain Greek yogurt

¼ cup (60 mL) extra virgin olive oil

1 teaspoon (5 mL) minced garlic

½ cup (125 mL) tahini (sesame butter)

¼ cup (60 mL) lemon juice

½ teaspoon (2.5 mL) cayenne pepper

Salt and pepper, to taste

For garnish

Fresh cilantro leaves

Edamame beans

Sesame seeds

METHOD

1. In a food processor, add all the ingredients except the salt and pepper, and process until smooth.
2. Season with salt and pepper. Transfer to a serving bowl and garnish as desired.

Nutritional value (per serving)
Calories: 408 Total fat: 35.1 g Saturated fats: 4.9 g Cholesterol: 0 mg
Sodium: 49 mg Carbohydrates: 15 g Fibers: 6 g Protein: 13 g

Yogurt Pearls

The next recipe isn't a recipe, really, but rather a tip that, once you know it, you won't be able to live without. The following simple instructions will allow you to create small frozen pearls of yogurt that can be used in all types of sorbet or frozen dessert recipes. The pearls can even be enjoyed as a snack or for dessert, as a substitute for ice cream over a piece of cake, or simply sprinkled over a mountain of fresh fruit. Thanks to this recipe, you'll have frozen yogurt on hand at all times! Moreover, because of their small size, the pearls are much easier to process than a big chunk of frozen yogurt is, making it easier for you to whip up frozen yogurt recipes.

 2 servings   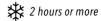 5 minutes   ❄ 2 hours or more

INGREDIENT
1 cup (250 mL) plain Greek yogurt

METHOD
1. Line a baking sheet with parchment paper.
2. Transfer the yogurt to a pastry bag fitted with a round tip, and create yogurt "pearls" on the parchment-lined baking sheet.
3. Freeze for about 2 hours, then transfer the yogurt pearls to an airtight container or resealable bag for future use.

Hubert's Tip: *You can add all sorts of different flavors to yogurt pearls. Let your imagination run free! You can also sweeten them by adding honey, maple syrup, agave syrup, or grenadine syrup. Lastly, you can mix Greek yogurt and pureed fresh fruit together to flavor the pearls.*

Nutritional value (per serving)
Calories: 87 Total fat: 2.5 g Saturated fats: 1.4 g Cholesterol: 11 mg
Sodium: 46 mg Carbohydrates: 4 g Fibers: 1 g Protein: 11 g

Grilled Pineapple

Pineapple is an extremely sweet fruit. Once grilled in a cast-iron skillet, it becomes even tastier.
I like to serve grilled pineapple with plain yogurt to reach the perfect balance of flavors.
This recipe is perfect for all kids, young and old alike.

4 servings   10 minutes   10 minutes

INGREDIENTS

1 whole pineapple

10 to 12 cardamom seeds

¼ cup (60 mL) maple syrup or honey

Fresh basil leaves, to taste

2 cups (500 mL) plain Greek yogurt

METHOD

1. Peel and core the pineapple. Cut the flesh lengthwise into 20 thin slices. Transfer the pineapple slices to paper towels to dry.

2. Grill the pineapple slices in a cast-iron skillet or on the barbecue, turning once.

3. Use a mortar and pestle to crush the cardamom seeds.

4. Whisk the crushed cardamom into the maple syrup or honey.

5. Brush the spiced syrup over the grilled pineapple slices.

6. Chop the basil leaves and sprinkle over the pineapple slices.

7. Serve five slices of pineapple and ½ cup (125 mL) Greek yogurt per person.

Nutritional value (per serving)
Calories: 201   Total fat: 2.7 g   Saturated fats: 1.4 g   Cholesterol: 11 mg
Sodium: 49 mg   Carbohydrates: 34 g   Fibers: 2 g   Protein: 12 g

The Perfect Frosted Raspberries

Summertime is a great time to cook lighter dishes. This snack is extremely fresh and versatile. You can enjoy the frosted raspberries on their own, sprinkle them over dessert, add them to a smoothie, or serve them with pancakes.

150 frosted raspberries   20 minutes   ❄ 4 hours

INGREDIENTS

¾ cup (180 mL) vanilla Greek yogurt

1 teaspoon (5 mL) rose water

150 fresh raspberries (about 2 pints)

METHOD

1. In a bowl, combine the yogurt and rose water.

2. Transfer the mixture to a pastry bag fitted with a round tip.

3. Pipe some of the yogurt mixture into each raspberry cavity.

4. Place the filled raspberries on a baking sheet and freeze for about 4 hours.

5. Transfer to an airtight container or resealable plastic bag, and enjoy immediately.

Hubert's Tip: *Eating seven portions of yogurt per week (one per day) lowers the risk of obesity by 12 percent. The risk is even lower for those who eat a lot of fruit.[9] Frosted raspberries are therefore the perfect snack!*

Nutritional value (for about 15 raspberries)
Calories: 26 Total fat: 0.5 g Saturated fats: 0.2 g Cholesterol: 1 mg
Sodium: 6 mg Carbohydrates: 4 g Fibers: 2 g Protein: 2 g

Creamy Fruit Salad

Who said eating fruit was boring? It's true that finding new ways to eat common foods helps you appreciate them more. This fruit salad is fresh, creamy, crunchy (yes! thanks to the addition of water chestnuts), and whimsical.

6 servings   5 minutes

INGREDIENTS
1 red apple, diced

1 pear, diced

1 nectarine, diced

2 kiwifruits, diced

1 cup (250 mL) strawberries, diced

¼ cup (60 mL) raspberries

¼ cup (60 mL) blackberries

½ cucumber, peeled, cored, and cubed

One 7.8-ounce (227 mL) can water chestnuts, diced

2 tablespoons (30 mL) coconut milk (see note)

¼ cup (60 mL) vanilla yogurt

1 cup (250 mL) miniature marshmallows

METHOD
1. Combine all the fruits, the cucumber, and the water chestnuts in a large mixing bowl.

2. In a separate bowl, combine the coconut milk with the yogurt and marshmallows. Transfer the sauce to the fruit mixture and stir to combine.

3. Serve immediately.

Note: Use only the solidified part of the coconut milk. Use the remaining liquid in smoothies or freeze it into cubes.

Nutritional value (per serving)
Calories: 158 Total fat: 5.3 g Saturated fats: 4.2 g Cholesterol: 1 mg
Sodium: 17 mg Carbohydrates: 29 g Fibers: 4 g Protein: 1 g

Cracker Jack

Popcorn is a great snack. You can flavor it many different ways, but I had the bold idea to dip it in Greek yogurt and confectioners' sugar and then bake it to see how it would turn out. The crispy and sweet creation tastes like Cracker Jack! It's a surprising but scrumptious result.

8 servings   10 minutes   15 minutes

INGREDIENTS

1 cup (250 mL) vanilla Greek yogurt

2½ cups (625 mL) confectioners' sugar

8 cups (2 L) plain popcorn

METHOD

1. Preheat the oven to 350°F (180°C).
2. In a large bowl, whisk the Greek yogurt and confectioners' sugar together.
3. Add the popcorn and fold to coat with the yogurt mixture.
4. Line a baking sheet with parchment paper. Spread the popcorn over the baking sheet.
5. Bake for 15 minutes, tossing the popcorn every 5 minutes.

Hubert's Tip: *Most lactose-intolerant teenagers and adults can ingest up to 12 grams (0.4 ounces) of lactose in one meal with no discomfort. This means that they can incorporate more dairy products in their diets if they make sure to distribute the consumption of such products throughout the day.*[10, 11]

Nutritional value (per serving)
Calories: 179   Total fat: 1 g   Saturated fats: 0.3 g   Cholesterol: 3 mg
Sodium: 10 mg   Carbohydrates: 41 g   Fibers: 1 g   Protein: 3 g

Baked Mini-Donuts

My grandmother was a fantastic cook. Cooking was her passion! She loved to make mini-donuts when we came to visit. My brother always liked dredging his donuts in confectioners' sugar, whereas I liked them plain. It's all a question of taste. Here I've adapted my grandmother's recipe, making it healthier by avoiding the frying process.

 24 mini-donuts · 15 minutes · 15 minutes

INGREDIENTS

¾ cup (180 mL) all-purpose flour

1 teaspoon (5 mL) baking powder

½ teaspoon (2.5 mL) freshly grated nutmeg

¼ teaspoon (1 mL) salt

1 egg

1 teaspoon (5 mL) lemon extract

⅓ cup (80 mL) granulated sugar

2 tablespoons (30 mL) canola oil

¼ cup (60 mL) almond milk

¼ cup (60 mL) vanilla Greek yogurt

Confectioners' sugar (optional)

METHOD

1. Preheat the oven to 350°F (180°C).

2. Butter the 24 cavities of a mini-donut mold.

3. In a mixing bowl, combine the flour, baking powder, nutmeg, and salt. Set aside.

4. In another bowl, whisk the egg, lemon extract, and sugar until the mixture is frothy, then add the canola oil.

5. Combine the dry ingredients with the wet ingredients, alternating with the almond milk and yogurt, and mix until the batter is smooth.

6. Transfer the batter to a pastry bag fitted with a round tip, and pipe the batter into the mini-donut cavities.

7. Bake for 15 minutes or until the donuts are golden.

8. Let cool slightly, then dredge in confectioners' sugar, if desired.

Nutritional value (for 2 mini-donuts)
Calories: 83   Total fat: 3.1 g   Saturated fats: 0.4 g   Cholesterol: 16 mg
Sodium: 117 mg   Carbohydrates: 12 g   Fibers: 0 g   Protein: 2 g

Energy Balls

Mid-afternoon cravings occur when you need an energy boost. These energy balls, rich in carbohydrates provided by banana and dried fruit, will give you just the kick you need to keep on going. I like to nibble on one or two of these while sipping a good cup of coffee.

12 balls   *15 minutes*

INGREDIENTS

½ banana

½ cup (125 mL) Greek yogurt, strained (see instructions on p. 19)

¾ cup (180 mL) rolled oats

1 cup (250 mL) dried figs

2 tablespoons (30 mL) chia seeds

2 tablespoons (30 mL) sunflower seeds

Three 1-ounce (10 g each) squares dark chocolate, grated

1 teaspoon (5 mL) vanilla extract

Pinch of salt

¼ cup (60 mL) macadamia nuts, chopped

METHOD

1. In the bowl of a food processor, add all the ingredients except the macadamia nuts, and process to create a lumpy dough.

2. Mix in the macadamia nuts. Scoop about 2 tablespoons (30 mL) of dough and roll into balls. Place the balls on a parchment-lined baking sheet and freeze for 15 minutes.

3. Once the balls are firm, transfer them to an airtight container and keep refrigerated. The energy balls will last in the fridge for 3 to 4 days (although there are never any leftovers when I make them!).

Nutritional value (for 1 ball)
Calories: 89   Total fat: 4.6 g   Saturated fats: 0.7 g   Cholesterol: 1 mg
Sodium: 4 mg   Carbohydrates: 10 g   Fibers: 2 g   Protein: 3 g

Orange and Almond Scones

Scones are small leavened buns hailing from Great Britain, where the traditional recipe passes down from generation to generation. Sweet scones are usually served with coffee or tea. What I like most about this recipe is that the small size of the scones makes them perfect for a snack. Plus, the combination of orange and almond flavors is nothing short of delightful.

 12 small scones   20 minutes 20 minutes

INGREDIENTS

½ cup (125 mL) orange juice, freshly squeezed

⅓ cup (80 mL) plain Greek yogurt

½ cup (125 mL) granulated sugar

¼ cup (60 mL) butter, melted

2 tablespoons (30 mL) orange zest

1 egg

½ teaspoon (2.5 mL) Grand Marnier

1½ cups (375 mL) all-purpose flour

1½ cups (375 mL) almond flour (ground almonds)

Pinch of salt

Whole almonds (optional, for garnish)

METHOD

1. Preheat the oven to 375°F (190°C).
2. In a large mixing bowl, combine the orange juice, yogurt, sugar, butter, orange zest, egg, and Grand Marnier.
3. In a second mixing bowl, combine the flour, almond flour, and salt.
4. Gradually add the dry ingredients into the wet ingredients, and mix until the dough is smooth.
5. Transfer the dough to a 12-cavity silicone baking mold.
6. Press three almonds onto each scone, if using.
7. Bake for 20 minutes or until the edges of the scones are lightly golden.
8. Let cool completely before unmolding.

Nutritional value (for 1 scone)
Calories: 205 Total fat: 6.8 g Saturated fats: 3 g Cholesterol: 27 mg
Sodium: 10 mg Carbohydrates: 29 g Fibers: 1 g Protein: 8 g

Goat Cheese, Grape, and Pecan Balls

It's easy to draw a blank when it comes to figuring out what to serve with a glass of wine during happy hour. Baguette is out, isn't it? And grapes on their own are nothing original. One day a friend served these goat cheese, grape, and pecan balls, and I fell in love. They've been the highlight of my happy hours ever since.

12 balls   10 minutes

INGREDIENTS

12 large green grapes

⅓ cup (80 mL) Greek yogurt, strained (see instructions on p. 19)

3 ounces (90 g) goat cheese

Finely chopped pecans (enough to cover all the balls)

METHOD

1. Rinse the grapes under cold water.
2. In a small bowl, mix the yogurt and goat cheese together.
3. Cover each grape with some of the yogurt and goat cheese mixture to create small balls.
4. Place the chopped pecans in a shallow plate.
5. Roll the balls in the pecans to cover completely.

Nutritional value (for 2 balls)
Calories: 366 Fat: 35.7 g Saturated fats: 5.9 g Cholesterol: 13 mg
Sodium: 83 mg Carbohydrates: 8 g Fibers: 4 g Protein: 8 g

Avocado Lassi

This drink is extremely popular in Vietnam, where fresh produce abounds. At the market, you'll find an endless supply of plump mangos and avocados. Avocado lassi has a lovely silky texture thanks to rich avocados and velvety mangos. But above all, it's a refreshing drink that comes together in minutes. You can serve avocado lassi as a snack or as a side dish to a meal.

2 servings   *5 minutes*

INGREDIENTS

2 ripe avocados

½ mango

1 cup (250 mL) almond milk

½ cup (125 mL) plain Greek yogurt

2 tablespoons (30 mL) granulated sugar or honey

½ teaspoon (2.5 mL) grated fresh ginger

1 cup (250 mL) ice cubes

METHOD

1. Blend all the ingredients, except the ice cubes, until the mixture is smooth.
2. Serve the avocado lassi in tall glasses filled with ice cubes.

Hubert's Tip: *A study has shown that the thicker a beverage is, the less people will drink of it. This result was observed in women research subjects only.[12] Both this avocado lassi and the Healthy Exotic Bowl with Dragon Fruit and Lychee recipe featured on page 42 are therefore outstanding healthy choices, specifically because of their rich texture.*

Nutritional value (per serving)
Calories: 368   Total fat: 23.6 g   Saturated fats: 3.7 g   Cholesterol: 5 mg
Sodium: 115 mg   Carbohydrates: 36 g   Fibers: 11 g   Protein: 9 g

Crunchy Corn Guacamole

As I've mentioned earlier, Mexican food is one of my favorite cuisines, and guacamole is probably my top choice in that cuisine. My recipe features a surprising but delightful combination: avocado and corn. Corn provides crunch, and avocado makes the dip velvety. This recipe is so delicious that I eat it by the spoonful, but it's just as perfect as an accompaniment to fajitas or with corn tortilla chips.

4 servings   *10 minutes*

INGREDIENTS

2 ripe avocados

½ cup (125 mL) plain Greek yogurt (0% milk fat)

¼ cup (60 mL) corn kernels, plus more for garnish

¼ cup (60 mL) finely chopped onion

¼ cup (60 mL) chopped fresh cilantro, plus more for garnish

3 tablespoons (45 mL) lime juice

¼ teaspoon (1 mL) ground cumin

Salt and pepper, to taste

METHOD

1. In a bowl, mash the avocados with a fork.

2. Mix in the yogurt.

3. Add the corn, onion, cilantro, lime juice, and cumin.

4. Season with salt and pepper to taste, mix well, garnish with additional corn and cilantro, and serve.

Nutritional value (per serving)
Calories: 201   Total fat: 15.5 g   Saturated fats: 2.5 g   Cholesterol: 3 mg
Sodium: 20 mg   Carbohydrates: 14 g   Fibers: 8 g   Protein: 5 g

Yogurt, Pistachio, and Freeze-Dried Fruit Bars

Yogurt freezes really well. However, because of its low fat content, it can become extremely hard once frozen, as opposed to ice cream, which remains spoonable. But why wouldn't you take advantage of that property to turn yogurt into frozen bars? After the mixture has been in the freezer for a few hours, all you need to do is break it into pieces and enjoy. Use your favorite nuts and fresh, canned, or dried fruits.

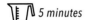 8 servings   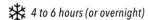 5 minutes   ❄ 4 to 6 hours (or overnight)

INGREDIENTS

3 cups (750 mL) vanilla Greek yogurt

¼ cup (60 mL) shelled and coarsely chopped unsalted pistachios

Freeze-dried pineapple, to taste

Freeze-dried strawberries, to taste

METHOD

1. Line a baking sheet with parchment paper.

2. Spread the yogurt in an even layer (about ¼-inch/6 mm thick) over the parchment paper.

3. Sprinkle with pistachios and dried and freeze-dried fruits to taste.

4. Freeze 4 to 6 hours, or overnight.

5. Break the frozen yogurt unto chunks and keep frozen in an airtight, resealable bag.

Hubert's Tip:
Flavor combination ideas:
- *Pistachios, dried cranberries*
- *Chopped almonds, cherries, goji berries*
- *Cashews, blackberries, white chocolate chips*
- *Coconut flakes, dark chocolate shavings, dried pineapple*
- *Homemade granola, raspberries, cinnamon sugar*
- *Pecans, caramel bits*
- *Basil, strawberries, lemon zest, pretzel sticks*

Nutritional value (per serving)
Calories: 125   Total fat: 3.4 g   Saturated fats: 1.1 g   Cholesterol: 8 mg
Sodium: 28 mg   Carbohydrates: 16 g   Fibers: 1 g   Protein: 9 g

5
Dessert

Amaretto and Espresso Cake

My infatuation for almond paste dates back many years. As a kid, I would go shopping with my parents, and I was obsessed by the creations on display at the pastry shop. I would have given anything to leave with a Winnie the Pooh made out of almond paste! Although I use almond paste in my own desserts now, I admit that I still have the same fascination for pastry shop displays.

 16 servings   15 minutes   30 minutes

INGREDIENTS

3 eggs

¼ cup (60 mL) plain Greek yogurt

¾ cup (180 mL) granulated sugar

⅓ cup (80 mL) butter, melted

½ cup (125 mL) almond paste

1 tablespoon (15 mL) amaretto

1 tablespoon (15 mL) espresso

1 cup (250 mL) all-purpose flour

1 teaspoon (5 mL) ground coffee

METHOD

1. Preheat the oven to 325°F (160°C).
2. Using an electric mixer, combine the eggs, yogurt, sugar, butter, almond paste, amaretto, and espresso, and beat until the mixture is smooth.
3. Incorporate the flour and ground coffee.
4. Transfer the mixture to a 9-inch (23 cm) square baking pan, then bake for 30 minutes.
5. Let cool completely, then cut into 16 squares.

Nutritional value (per serving)
Calories: 163   Total fat: 7.8 g   Saturated fats: 3.3 g   Cholesterol: 50 mg
Sodium: 16 mg   Carbohydrates: 20 g   Fibers: 1 g   Protein: 3 g

Passion Fruit Panna Cotta

It was inconceivable for me not to include a panna cotta recipe in this book, but I wanted the recipe to be colorful, exotic, and different. I think this dessert spells mission accomplished: the custard unveils a touch of spice coming from the jalapeño-infused cream, and that surprising flavor is then tamed by the freshness of tropical passion fruit.

 4 servings   20 minutes   5 minutes   2 hours or more

INGREDIENTS

One ¼-ounce (7 g) packet gelatin

¼ cup (60 mL) cold water

2 cups (500 mL) vanilla Greek yogurt

1 cup (250 mL) milk, divided

1 cup (250 mL) whipping cream (35% milk fat), divided

¼ cup (60 mL) + 2 tablespoons (30 mL) granulated sugar

1 jalapeño pepper, cut into pieces

2 tablespoons (30 mL) lemon juice

4 passion fruits

METHOD

1. Sprinkle the gelatin over the cold water and let rest for 15 minutes.

2. In a large mixing bowl, combine the yogurt, half the milk, and half the cream.

3. In a small saucepan, bring the rest of the milk and cream to a simmer, then add ¼ cup (60 mL) sugar and the jalapeño pepper.

4. Remove from the heat and discard the jalapeño pepper.

5. Whisk the gelatin into the hot mixture (the gelatin should dissolve completely).

6. Combine the warm mixture with the cold yogurt mixture, and mix well. Add the lemon juice.

7. Divide the custard among four ramekins or glasses, and refrigerate for at least 2 hours.

8. Scoop the flesh out of the passion fruits, and transfer to a nonstick skillet set over medium heat. Add 2 tablespoons (30 mL) sugar and whisk continuously for about 5 to 7 minutes.

9. Serve the panna cotta drizzled with the passion fruit syrup.

Nutritional value (per serving)
Calories: 190 Total fat: 3.6 g Saturated fats: 1.7 g Cholesterol: 16 mg
Sodium: 103 mg Carbohydrates: 24 g Fibers: 1 g Protein: 16 g

Brownie Bites

Brownies rank high on my list of favorite desserts, but I'm very picky as to which ones bring me the most pleasure. I love those that are soft and super chocolatey, and my recipe creates just such a brownie. My secrets are to make them bite-sized and to make sure not to overcook them.

30 bites   10 minutes   7 to 8 minutes

INGREDIENTS

¾ cup (180 mL) all-purpose flour

½ cup (125 mL) cocoa powder

½ teaspoon (2.5 mL) salt

¼ teaspoon (1 mL) baking soda

1 cup (250 mL) brown sugar

½ cup (125 mL) unsweetened applesauce

½ cup (125 mL) plain Greek yogurt

2 ounces (60 g) chocolate chips (or dark chocolate chunks), melted

2 large eggs

2 tablespoons (30 mL) vegetable oil

METHOD

1. Preheat the oven to 350°F (180°C).

2. In a mixing bowl, combine the flour, cocoa powder, salt, and baking soda.

3. In another bowl, combine the brown sugar, applesauce, yogurt, melted chocolate, eggs, and vegetable oil.

4. Using a spatula, gradually fold the dry ingredients into the wet ingredients.

5. Pour the batter into mini-muffin cups or mini-financier molds, and bake for 7 to 8 minutes.

Hubert's Tip: *You can also bake these brownies in an 8-inch (20 cm) square dish, but make sure to increase the cooking time to 30 to 35 minutes.*

Nutritional value (for 3 bites)
Calories: 191 Total fat: 6.4 g Saturated fats: 1.9 g Cholesterol: 41 mg
Sodium: 59 mg Carbohydrates: 31 g Fibers: 2 g Protein: 5 g

Fleur de Sel Caramel

A good friend of mine has generously given me the secret to her mother's salted caramel. It's so delicious; once you taste it, you're left only wanting more. It's the perfect homemade gift for friends, coworkers, or neighbors. If you manage to keep some for yourself, enjoy it drizzled over apple slices or yogurt. It's a real treat!

 8 servings   5 minutes   5 minutes

INGREDIENTS

¼ cup (60 mL) water

1 cup (250 mL) granulated sugar

½ cup (125 mL) whipping cream (35% milk fat)

½ teaspoon (2.5 mL) fleur de sel

¼ cup (60 mL) unsalted butter, diced

Pistachios, for garnish

To serve

Plain Greek yogurt

Apple slices

METHOD

1. In a saucepan, bring the water and sugar to a boil. Cook, without stirring, until the mixture turns golden. Keep an eye on it, though, as it can burn quickly.

2. As soon as the mixture is golden, remove from the heat and whisk in the cream and fleur de sel.

3. Add the cubed butter, and mix until the butter is completely melted.

4. Let cool.

5. Garnish with pistachios, and serve with apple slices and plain Greek yogurt.

Nutritional value (per serving of caramel sauce)
Calories: 207 Total fat: 11.6 g Saturated fats: 7.3 g Cholesterol: 36 mg
Sodium: 7 mg Carbohydrates: 27 g Fibers: 0 g Protein: 0 g

Key Lime Tartlets with Speculoos Crusts

One of my summer guilty pleasures is to make individual-sized lemon or lime pies and serve them to my guests during a barbecue or a dinner party. This dessert looks light, but it tastes decadent. As a substitute for graham crackers, I use crushed speculoos cookies for the crust, which lends a spectacular result. Trust me: one tartlet won't be enough!

🍴 4 tartlets   🥤 25 minutes   🧤 2 hours and 25 minutes total   🌡 1 hour

INGREDIENTS

For the crust

¼ cup (60 mL) butter, melted

About 20 speculoos cookies, crushed

1 tablespoon (15 mL) lime zest

For the filling

1 cup (250 mL) plain Greek yogurt

½ cup (125 mL) granulated sugar

2 eggs

½ cup (125 mL) lime juice

1 tablespoon (15 mL) lime zest

For the meringues

3 egg whites

1 teaspoon (5 mL) cream of tartar

¾ cup (180 mL) granulated sugar

Hubert's Tip: *Adding lime zest to the crust amplifies the citrus flavor of these tartlets.*

METHOD

1. Preheat the oven to 350°F (180°C).

For the crust

2. In a bowl, combine the butter, crushed speculoos, and lime zest. Press the mixture into four 4-inch (10 cm) tartlet molds.

3. Bake the crusts for 5 minutes, then let cool completely.

For the filling

4. In a large bowl, whisk the yogurt and sugar together. Add the eggs, one at a time, whisking continuously. Incorporate the lime juice and zest.

5. Divide the filling between the crusts and bake for 20 minutes or until the center is almost set (the filling should remain slightly jiggly; it will firm up as it cools).

6. Let cool, then refrigerate for at least 1 hour before topping with meringues and serving.

For the meringues

7. Preheat the oven to 175°F (80°C).

8. Whisk the egg whites and cream of tartar together. Then, with an electric mixer, beat until soft peaks form. Add the sugar, then keep on beating on high speed until stiff peaks form.

9. Line a baking sheet with parchment paper.

10. Transfer the meringue to a pastry bag fitted with a round or star tip, and pipe small meringues onto the parchment paper.

11. Bake for 2 hours, then turn the oven off and let the meringues cool completely in the oven.

12. Serve the tartlets topped with meringues.

Nutritional value (for 1 tartlet)
Calories: 607 Total fat: 17.8 g Saturated fats: 8.5 g Cholesterol: 129 mg
Sodium: 326 mg Carbohydrates: 101 g Fibers: 2 g Protein: 14 g

Yogurt, Berry, and Green Tea Mousse

One of my goals for this book was to create the perfect fruity and healthy dessert. I think I succeeded! This green tea–flavored mousse reminds me of summer. You could serve it as a light dessert for brunch or as a refreshing snack on a hot afternoon.

4 servings   30 minutes   3 hours or more

INGREDIENTS

1 bag green tea

1 teaspoon (5 mL) honey

Two ¼-ounce (7 g) packets gelatin, divided

1½ cups (375 mL) mixed berries

1⅓ cups (320 mL) vanilla Greek yogurt

1 teaspoon (5 mL) rose water

METHOD

1. Infuse the green tea in 1 cup (250 mL) boiling water for 3 minutes.
2. Whisk in the honey and one of the gelatin packets.
3. Cut out four 3- × 10-inch (8 × 25 cm) rectangles from acetate sheets (see note).
4. Line the interior walls of four ramekins with the acetate rectangles.
5. Press the berries into the bottom of the ramekins.
6. Pour some of the green tea on top to cover the berries completely.
7. Refrigerate for 2 hours or until the berry and green tea layer is set.
8. In a bowl, combine the yogurt, rose water, and remaining gelatin packet.
9. Pour this mixture over the berry and green tea layer, and refrigerate for 1 hour (or overnight) to set.
10. Serve cold, garnished with fresh fruit.

Note: You can find acetate sheets at specialty baking stores. Their firmness will help you remove the mousse from the ramekins after you've refrigerated it.

Nutritional value (per serving)
Calories: 94   Total fat: 1.8 g   Saturated fats: 0.9 g   Cholesterol: 7 mg
Sodium: 37 mg   Carbohydrates: 9 g   Fibers: 2 g   Protein: 11 g

Dark Beer Whoopie Pies

My grandmother always made whoopie pies and molasses cookies when she knew we were coming to visit. Because she lived so far from my home, visiting her was like a celebration. Before I left to return home, she would always hand me a biscuit tin filled with her delicious creations. This recipe makes me nostalgic for those precious moments spent with my grandmother.

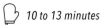 30 whoopie pies   40 minutes   10 to 13 minutes

INGREDIENTS

For the whoopie pies

1 cup (250 mL) dark beer

1 cup (250 mL) unsalted butter

½ cup (125 mL) cocoa powder

2 eggs

⅔ cup (160 mL) plain yogurt

2½ cups (625 mL) all-purpose flour

1½ cups (375 mL) granulated sugar

1½ teaspoons (7.5 mL) baking soda

½ teaspoon (2.5 mL) salt

For the filling

Two 8-ounce (226 g) packages light cream cheese

¾ cup (180 mL) vanilla Greek yogurt, strained (see instructions on p. 19)

1½ cups (375 mL) confectioners' sugar

METHOD

For the whoopie pies

1. Preheat the oven to 350°F (180°C).
2. Place the beer and butter in a saucepan, and bring to a boil. Whisk in the cocoa powder, and keep on whisking until the mixture is smooth. Let cool completely.
3. In a bowl, combine the eggs and yogurt. Add the cocoa mixture and mix until smooth.
4. Sift the flour, sugar, baking soda, and salt together, and fold into the wet ingredients using a spatula. Let the mixture rest for 10 minutes.
5. Working in batches, on a baking sheet lined with parchment paper, drop tablespoonfuls (15 mL) of dough, spacing each mound by 1 inch (2.5 cm). You should have 60 mounds total.
6. Bake for 10 to 13 minutes or until a toothpick inserted in one of the cookies comes out clean. Let cool completely.

For the filling

7. Using an electric mixer, beat the cream cheese and Greek yogurt together. At low speed, gradually incorporate the confectioners' sugar, then beat until the filling is smooth and light.

To assemble

8. Spread 1 to 2 tablespoons (15 to 30 mL) of filling onto the underside of a cookie, then sandwich with another cookie. Repeat to create all the whoopie pies.

Nutritional value (for 1 whoopie pie)
Calories: 218   Total fat: 10.1 g   Saturated fats: 6 g   Cholesterol: 40 mg
Sodium: 153 mg   Carbohydrates: 28 g   Fibers: 1 g   Protein: 4 g

Creamy White Chocolate Dip

I can think of nothing better than getting together with friends around a chocolate fondue. It's a simple thing to prepare, too: simply dice your favorite fresh fruits and serve them with a bowl of melted chocolate. This recipe is a twist on that fun classic: it mixes yogurt with white chocolate. The result is super creamy and rich and is an excellent dipping vehicle for any and all types of fruit.

8 servings   15 minutes   1 hour

INGREDIENTS

1 cup (250 mL) white chocolate chips

¼ cup (60 mL) whipping cream (35% milk fat)

½ cup (125 mL) Greek yogurt (2% milk fat)

½ teaspoon (2.5 mL) agar-agar powder

Fresh fruit

METHOD

1. Melt the white chocolate in a double boiler.
2. In a bowl, whisk the cream and yogurt together.
3. Slowly pour the melted white chocolate into the cream and yogurt mixture, whisking to combine.
4. Whisk in the agar-agar.
5. Refrigerate for 1 hour.
6. Serve with diced fresh fruit.

Nutritional value (per serving)
Calories: 170   Total fat: 10.2 g   Saturated fats: 6.1 g   Cholesterol: 14 mg
Sodium: 30 mg   Carbohydrates: 18 g   Fibers: 0 g   Protein: 3 g

Layered Apples

Of all the desserts I'm sharing in this book, this one is probably my favorite. Slicing apples thinly using a mandolin allows you to fold them taco-style, making the dessert extremely easy to eat. The trick is to make sure you catch a bit of crumble and some yogurt with every bite. The vanilla bean pod is an essential component of this dish. However, if you don't have vanilla beans at home, you can replace them with freshly grated nutmeg.

4 servings   15 minutes   15 minutes   25 minutes

INGREDIENTS

For the granola

⅓ cup (80 mL) walnuts

¼ cup (60 mL) slivered almonds

½ cup (125 mL) almond flour (ground almonds)

⅓ cup (80 mL) rolled oats

¼ cup (60 mL) brown sugar

¼ cup (60 mL) butter, melted

For the yogurt cream

⅓ cup (80 mL) vanilla yogurt (10% milk fat)

½ cup (125 mL) whipping cream (35% milk fat)

1 vanilla pod

To serve

1 Granny Smith apple

1 red apple

Water

Juice from 1 lemon

Basil leaves

METHOD

For the granola

1. Preheat the oven to 350°F (180°C).
2. In a large mixing bowl, combine the walnuts, slivered almonds, almond flour, rolled oats, brown sugar, and melted butter.
3. Line a baking sheet with parchment paper.
4. Transfer the granola mixture to the baking sheet, using your fingers to create chunks.
5. Bake for 25 minutes, tossing the granola halfway through, until it's golden.
6. Turn the oven off and leave the granola in the oven to dry for 15 minutes with the door ajar.

For the yogurt cream

7. In a large mixing bowl, combine the yogurt, cream, and seeds from the vanilla bean.

To assemble

8. Use a mandolin to slice both apples thinly. Remove the seeds.
9. Dip the apple slices in a bowl of water mixed with lemon juice so they don't brown.
10. On a serving plate, stack up the apple slices, sprinkle with granola, and top with the yogurt cream and basil. Serve immediately.

Nutritional value (per serving)
Calories: 330   Total fat: 25 g   Saturated fats: 8.1 g   Cholesterol: 39 mg
Sodium: 22 mg   Carbohydrates: 20 g   Fibers: 2 g   Protein: 10 g

Coffee Semifreddo

Semifreddo is an Italian dessert that is healthy and never fails to create a wow effect. You can go wild with the presentation of the dish! Those who know me know that I can't live a day without coffee: I just love its aroma. It was obvious this book had to have one recipe with coffee as its star ingredient. Enjoy!

12 servings *20 minutes* *6 to 8 hours*

INGREDIENTS

4 egg whites

½ teaspoon (2.5 mL) cream of tartar

¾ cup (180 mL) granulated sugar

1½ cups (375 mL) vanilla Greek yogurt

½ cup (125 mL) plain, high-fat yogurt

Pinch of salt

Juice from 1 lemon

Raspberries (about 60 berries)

3 tablespoons (45 mL) ground coffee

For garnish

Cocoa powder

Chocolate shavings

Coffee beans

METHOD

1. In a large mixing bowl, whisk the egg whites and cream of tartar together.
2. With an electric mixer, beat until soft peaks form. Add the sugar and keep on beating on high speed until stiff peaks form. Set aside.
3. In a separate large mixing bowl, combine both yogurts, salt and the lemon juice, then add a third of the beaten egg whites. Mix to incorporate fully. Fold in the rest of the egg whites using a spatula.
4. Line a loaf pan with parchment paper, and allow some of the paper to hang over the sides for easy removal of the dessert later.
5. Pour a third of the yogurt and egg white mixture into the bottom of the pan.
6. Cover with raspberries.
7. Combine the ground coffee with the remaining yogurt and egg white mixture, and pour into the pan.
8. Freeze for at least 6 hours.
9. To unmold, dip the bottom of the pan into hot water for a few seconds. Invert the pan onto a serving plate.
10. Garnish the semifreddo with cocoa powder, chocolate shavings, and coffee beans.

Nutritional value (per serving)
Calories: 106 Total fat: 1.3 g Saturated fats: 0.7 g Cholesterol: 5 mg
Sodium: 33 mg Carbohydrates: 20 g Fibers: 1 g Protein: 4 g

Banana, Walnut, and Toblerone Bread

This Toblerone-filled banana bread goes well with a creamy latte or cappuccino, and is a delicious treat. When your bananas are past ripe, don't throw them away! It's the perfect time to freeze them or add them to an aromatic quick bread. Don't forget to add nuts to increase the protein, good fats, and fiber content.

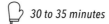 12 slices   15 minutes   30 to 35 minutes

INGREDIENTS

½ cup (125 mL) unsalted butter

1 cup (250 mL) granulated sugar

2 eggs

1 teaspoon (5 mL) vanilla extract

2 very ripe bananas

¼ cup (60 mL) plain Greek yogurt

1 cup (250 mL) all-purpose flour

½ cup (125 mL) whole wheat flour

1 teaspoon (5 mL) baking soda

Pinch of salt

1 cup (250 mL) chopped walnuts

½ cup (125 mL) chopped Toblerone chocolate

1 banana (optional, for garnish)

METHOD

1. Preheat the oven to 350°F (180°C).
2. In a large bowl, whisk the butter and sugar together.
3. Add the eggs, one at a time, then mix in the vanilla extract, bananas, and yogurt.
4. In another bowl, combine the flours, baking soda, and salt.
5. Gradually incorporate the dry ingredients into the wet ingredients. Using an electric mixer, mix at low speed to combine thoroughly.
6. Fold the walnuts and Toblerone chunks into the batter, then pour it into a loaf pan lined with parchment paper.
7. If you wish, slice a banana lengthwise (or in rounds) and set over the batter, pressing on the banana slices so they sink slightly into the batter.
8. Bake for 30 to 35 minutes. For a semi-cooked bread, subtract 5 minutes from the cooking time.

Hubert's Tip: *Did you know that walnuts are primarily made up of polyunsaturated fats? These good fats are beneficial to heart health. Don't hesitate to add them to your favorite recipes!*

Nutritional value (for 1 slice)
Calories: 336   Total fat: 17.3 g   Saturated fats: 7.4 g   Cholesterol: 56 mg
Sodium: 141 mg   Carbohydrates: 42 g   Fibers: 2 g   Protein: 6 g

Blueberry Cobbler

I'm a big fan of fruity desserts (though I do love chocolate, too!), but I like this one first and foremost because of how easy it is to make. You can bake it right in a cast-iron skillet, it's so simple! This recipe uses blueberries, but you can substitute the fruit of your choice.

 6 servings   10 minutes   20 minutes

INGREDIENTS

½ cup (125 mL) + 2 tablespoons (30 mL) all-purpose flour

1 teaspoon (5 mL) baking powder

1½ tablespoons (22.5 mL) + ½ cup (125 mL) granulated sugar

Freshly grated nutmeg

2 tablespoons (30 mL) butter, cubed

1 egg

¼ cup (60 mL) plain, high-fat Greek yogurt

2 cups (500 mL) blueberries

1 tablespoon (15 mL) orange zest

Juice from 1 orange

METHOD

1. Preheat the oven to 350°F (180°C).
2. In a large mixing bowl, combine ½ cup (125 mL) flour, baking powder, 1½ tablespoons (22.5 mL) sugar, and nutmeg.
3. Add the butter, egg, and yogurt, and mix with an electric mixer until the dough is smooth. Set aside.
4. In a 9-inch (23 cm) cast-iron skillet, combine the blueberries, 2 tablespoons (30 mL) flour, ½ cup (125 mL) sugar, the orange zest, and the orange juice. Cook over medium heat for a few minutes or until the mixture thickens. Remove from the heat.
5. Divide the yogurt dough into five to six mounds, then distribute over the fruit mixture.
6. Bake for 15 minutes.
7. Serve warm, topped with ice cream, yogurt, or whipped cream.

Nutritional value (per serving)
Calories: 210   Total fat: 5.9 g   Saturated fats: 3.2 g   Cholesterol: 44 mg
Sodium: 233 mg   Carbohydrates: 37 g   Fibers: 2 g   Protein: 4 g

Chocolate-Dipped Cheesecake Bites

My goal with this recipe was to make creative fine chocolates. So I thought up the idea of making a chocolate-dipped bite out of a classic cheesecake with a graham cracker crumb crust. How enticing does that sound? You can thank me later.

🍴 30 bites   🥛 20 minutes   🧤 50 minutes   🌡 2 hours

INGREDIENTS

For the crust

1¼ cups (310 mL) graham cracker crumbs

¼ cup (60 mL) butter, melted

For the filling

8 ounces (226 g) soft tofu

8 ounces (226 g) cream cheese

5 egg yolks

½ cup (125 mL) plain yogurt

3 tablespoons (45 mL) lemon juice

1 teaspoon (5 mL) vanilla extract

⅓ cup (80 mL) all-purpose flour, sifted

5 egg whites

⅔ cup (160 mL) confectioners' sugar

For the chocolate dip

10½ ounces (300 g) quality milk chocolate

3 tablespoons (45 mL) coconut oil

METHOD

For the crust

1. Preheat the oven to 350°F (180°C).
2. Combine the graham cracker crumbs and melted butter, then press the mixture into the bottom of a 9-inch (23 cm) springform pan to create the crust.
3. Bake the crust for 6 to 8 minutes. Let cool completely.

For the filling

4. In a food processor, add the tofu, cream cheese, egg yolks, yogurt, lemon juice, vanilla extract, and flour, and process until the mixture is smooth. Transfer the yogurt mixture to a large bowl.
5. In another bowl, make a meringue by beating the egg whites with the confectioners' sugar until soft peaks form.
6. Gently mix a third of the meringue into the yogurt mixture, then fold in the rest of the meringue into the mixture using a spatula.
7. Pour the mixture over the crust and bake for 45 minutes or until the top of the cake is golden.
8. Let cool to room temperature, then unmold and cut into small 1-inch (2.5 cm) squares.

For the chocolate dip

9. In a double boiler, melt the milk chocolate and coconut oil together, whisking constantly.
10. Using a fork, gently dip the cheesecake squares into the melted chocolate, making sure the chocolate covers each square completely.
11. Transfer the chocolate-covered squares onto a parchment-lined baking sheet and refrigerate for 2 hours before serving.

Nutritional value (for 2 bites)

Calories: 206   Total fat: 11.9 g   Saturated fats: 6 g   Cholesterol: 83 mg   Sodium: 126 mg   Carbohydrates: 20 g   Fibers: 1 g   Protein: 5 g

Pumpkin Spice Sorbet

Every fall, I eagerly await the return of the pumpkin spice chai latte season. I love that comforting drink, and I have to say–without being pretentious–that I make the very best version of it. It took me a great deal of practice to get there! In fact, I love that aromatic flavor so much that I've decided to turn it into an indulgent sorbet.

4 servings   *10 minutes*   *2 hours*

INGREDIENTS

1½ tablespoons (22.5 mL) pumpkin spice chai tea (or regular chai tea)

1 cup (250 mL) pumpkin puree

½ cup (125 mL) whipping cream (35% milk fat)

½ cup (125 mL) plain Greek yogurt

⅓ cup (80 mL) granulated sugar

Pinch of salt

METHOD

1. Using a mortar and pestle, crush the pumpkin spice chai tea into a powder.

2. In a food processor, combine the pumpkin puree, cream, yogurt, sugar, salt, and crushed chai tea.

3. Transfer to a glass dish. Freeze for 2 hours, stirring every 30 minutes to create a creamy consistency.

Hubert's Tip: *If you let the sorbet freeze for over 30 minutes without stirring it, it will set too hard and you won't be able to reach a smooth and creamy texture. If the sorbet is too firm, rest it at room temperature for a few minutes before mixing it as instructed.*

Nutritional value (per serving)
Calories: 217   Total fat: 11.9 g   Saturated fats: 7.4 g   Cholesterol: 43 mg
Sodium: 28 mg   Carbohydrates: 25 g   Fibers: 2 g   Protein: 4 g

Yogurt and Melon Pavlova

I've always loved art. Surprisingly, it's only when I started working on this book that
I noticed that art is everywhere around us. In the kitchen, you can create something spectacular
with just a few basic ingredients. To me, this pavlova is a work of art. I can't stop admiring
this dessert's bright white meringue and dazzling colors. What's more, it's just as
sublime in reality as it is on paper!

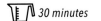 10 servings   30 minutes   2 hours

INGREDIENTS

For the pavlova

4 egg whites

Pinch of cream of tartar

1 cup (250 mL) granulated sugar

2 teaspoons (10 mL) cornstarch

1 teaspoon (5 mL) white vinegar

1 teaspoon (5 mL) coconut extract

For the topping

¾ cup (180 mL) vanilla Greek yogurt
(2% milk fat)

1 cup (250 mL) coconut milk (see
note)

¼ cup (60 mL) dried coconut flakes

Various melon varieties (canary,
cantaloupe, honeydew)

Papaya

Fresh mint leaves, for garnish

METHOD

For the pavlova

1. Preheat the oven to 175°F (80°C).
2. Trace an 8-inch (20 cm) circle on a piece of parchment
    paper and place it on a baking sheet.
3. Whisk the egg whites and cream of tartar together. Beat
    using an electric mixer until soft peaks form. Add the sugar
    and keep on beating on high speed until stiff peaks form.
4. Mix in the cornstarch, vinegar, and coconut extract.
5. Spread the meringue inside the traced circle on the
    parchment paper, creating a "nest" with higher sides and a
    sunken center to receive the filling.
6. Bake for 2 hours. Turn the oven off and let cool completely
    in the oven.
7. Add the topping 30 minutes before serving.

For the topping

8. In a large mixing bowl, combine the yogurt, coconut milk,
    and coconut flakes.
9. Spoon the mixture into the center of the cooled meringue.
10. Use a melon baller to create about 30 balls from the
    different melon varieties and papaya and carefully place
    them over the yogurt topping.
11. Garnish with fresh mint leaves and serve.

*Note: Use only the solidified part of the coconut milk. Use the remaining
liquid in smoothies or freeze it into cubes.*

Nutritional value (per serving)
Calories: 149   Total fat: 5.1 g   Saturated fats: 4.4 g   Cholesterol: 2 mg
Sodium: 31 mg   Carbohydrates: 24 g   Fibers: 1 g   Protein: 3 g

Notes

1. The Yogurt Council, The History of Yogurt, 2013.

2. N. Batmanglij, *A Taste of Persia: An Introduction to Persian Cooking* (I.B. Tauris, 2007).

3. J. Bostock and H.T. Riley, *The Natural History of Pliny* (London: Bell, 1856–93), 3:84.

4. *Encyclopaedia Britannica*, s.v. "Mahmud-Kashgari." Islam Etkisindeki Türk Edebiyati.

5. M.A. Veldhorst, A.G. Nieuwenhuizen, A. Hochstenbach-Waelen, et al., "Comparison of the Effects of a High- and Normal-Casein Breakfast on Satiety, 'Satiety' Hormones, Plasma Amino Acids and Subsequent Energy Intake," *British Journal of Nutrition* 101, no. 2 (2009): 295–303.

6. D. Mozaffarian, M.C. de Oliveira Otto, R.N. Lemaitre, et al., "Trans-Palmitoleic Acid, Other Dairy Fat Biomarkers, and Incident Diabetes: The Multi-Ethnic Study of Atherosclerosis (MESA)," *American Journal of Clinical Nutrition* 97, no. 4 (2013), doi:10.3945/ajcn.112.045468.

7. H. Cormier, É. Thifault, V. Garneau, et al., "Association between Yogurt Consumption, Dietary Patterns, and Cardio-Metabolic Risk Factors," *European Journal of Nutrition* 55, no. 2 (2015), doi:10.1007/s00394-015-0878-1.

8. P.F. Jacques and H. Wang, "Yogurt and Weight Management," *American Journal of Clinical Nutrition* 99 (2014): 1229S–34S.

9. M.A. Martinez-Gonzalez, C. Sayon-Orea, M. Ruiz-Canela, et al., "Yogurt Consumption, Weight Change and Risk of Overweight/Obesity: The SUN Cohort Study," *Nutrition, Metabolism, and Cardiovascular Diseases* 24, no. 11 (2014): 1189–96.

10. T.J. Wilt, A. Shaukat, T. Shamliyan, et al., "Lactose Intolerance and Health," *Evidence Reports/Technology Assessment*, no. 192 (2010): 1–410.

11. M.B. Heyman, "Lactose Intolerance in Infants, Children, and Adolescents," *Pediatrics* 118, no. 3 (2006): 1279–86.

12. K. McCrickerd, L. Chambers, and M.R. Yeomans, "Does Modifying the Thick Texture and Creamy Flavor of a Drink Change Portion Size Selection and Intake?" *Appetite*, no. 73 (2014): 114–20.

Acknowledgements

Writing a book is always a long process—and an unequalled opportunity for introspection. With *Yogurt Every Day*, I strived to outdo myself. I've always had a strong passion for cooking. I'm not a chef, and I haven't been formally trained as a cook, but I have been reading cookbooks and watching food television shows—from reality TV competitions to chef-driven series—since I was a kid. This is where my inspiration comes from. In this book, I wanted to create recipes that are healthy but without sacrificing taste or pleasure. Have I accomplished my mission? You tell me, but I'm extremely pleased with the results.

Recipes are great on their own, but when beautifully illustrated, they are infinitely better. I was extremely privileged to work with a multitalented food photographer for three weeks, during which time we snapped more than 75 recipes. Catherine Côté is quite simply an exceptional photographer. She has an amazing eye, both for aesthetics and details; she's truly a creator of mouthwatering atmospheres. I'm convinced that her pictures made you hungry. Even though I nearly set her loft on fire after an incredibly long day (no serious damage was caused!), I will remember our collaboration as one of the best experiences of my life. Catherine has tasted almost all the dishes featured in *Yogurt Every Day*. She loved them, and she's since decided she can't live without yogurt. Thank you, Catherine.

I am surrounded by many passionate people. Some of them helped me during the shooting of the recipes, and others lent a hand in the production of the book. I would like to send heartfelt thanks to Maude Fournier, Caroline Lamy, Marie-Ève Caplette, Jessica Vigneault, and Élisabeth Thifault for their time, which they offered without asking for anything in return. A very special thank you to Alexandra Laliberté, who helped me from the very beginning of this adventure.

I also want to thank Danielle Moore, Manon Cormier, and Anne-Marie Myers, who believed in me from the start. I'm infinitely grateful for your support, your ideas, and your open-mindedness.

Thanks to Appetite by Random House for trusting me to carry out this project, and more specifically, to my editor Zoe Maslow and my publisher Robert McCullough, two outstanding people.

Finally, I would like to thank my parents, who give me what's most precious in life: their unconditional love. Thank you for supporting all my projects and for always standing by me. I love you!

Index